Butterworth (Ireland) Guide to the European Communities

Butterworths
European Information Services

(Irish Editor : Aindrias O' Caoimh)

Butterworths
Dublin, London, Edinburgh, Munich
1989

Ireland	Butterworth (Ireland) Ltd, DUBLIN
Australia	Butterworths Pty Ltd, SYDNEY, MELBOURNE, BRISBANE, ADELAIDE, PERTH, CANBERRA and HOBART
Canada	Butterworths. A division of Reed Inc., TORONTO and VANCOUVER
Maylaysia	Malayan Law Journal Sdn Bhd, KUALA LUMPUR
New Zealand	Butterworths of New Zealand Ltd, WELLINGTON and AUCKLAND
Singapore	Butterworth & Co (Asia) Pte Ltd, SINGAPORE
United Kingdom	Butterworth & Co (Publishers) Ltd 88 Kingsway, LONDON WC2B 6AB 4 Hill Street, EDINBURGH EH2 3JZ
USA	Butterworths Legal Publishers, ST PAUL, Minnesota, SEATTLE, Washington, BOSTON, Massachusetts, AUSTIN, Texas and D & S Publishers, CLEARWATER, Florida

First Published 1989

A CIP catalogue record for this book is available from the British Library

© Butterworth (Ireland) Ltd

ISBN Paperback 1 85475 192 1.

Printed and bound in Great Britain by The Cotswold Group

PUBLISHER'S NOTE

As momentum gathers towards achieving the Single European Market, Community law is increasingly playing an important role in the work of lawyers, accountants, businessmen and students alike. The aim of this book is to make life a little easier by providing, in a concise and easy-to-follow format, the fundamental principles of Community law and a comprehensive reference source of important legislative provisions and judicial decisions which affect everyday problems.

The book is divided into four parts and states the law as at 25 April 1989.

Part I provides a chronology of events from 1947 to the present day highlighting the events leading up to the foundation of the European Communities and its development since; the aims and objects of the European Communities and the meaning and application of Community law.

Part II looks at the main institutions, their organisation and structure, procedure and location.

Part III considers all Community policies, each chapter following the same format detailing the relevant treaty provisions and secondary legislation, main principles and cases one should be aware of when faced with a problem in any specific area involving Community law.

Part IV is a fact file containing useful addresses, publications, glossary and abbreviations.

As the basis for Community law lies in the Treaty of Rome, as amended by the Single European Act, an Appendix containing the full amended text of the Treaty is included.

Any queries on the content or scope of this work should be directed to the Managing Editor, Butterworths European Information Services, at 88 Kingsway, London WC2B 6AB.

BUTTERWORTHS LAW PUBLISHERS LTD

CONTENTS

TABLES

EC PRIMARY LEGISLATION

EC SECONDARY LEGISLATION

References given in brackets refer to where the full text may be found in the Official Journal of the European Communities.

Directives etc.

OTHER PROVISIONS
Com Docs

Conventions

Statutes

SIs

CASES

A

Abels v Bedrijfsvereniging voor de Metaalindustrie en de Electrotechnische Industrie (135/83) [1987] 2 CMLR 406 **22.4**

Adoui and Cornuaille v Belgium (115, 116/81) [1982] ECR 1665 **12.5**

Anciens ELS d' Angenieux v Hauenberg (13/73) [1973] ECR 935 **12.6**

Anglo-Irish Meats v Minister for Agriculture(196/80) [1981] ECR 2263 **4.3**

B

Balkan Import-Export GmbH v Hauptzollamt Berlin-Packhof (5/73) [1973] ECR 1091 **21.3**

Beguelin Import v G L Import Export (22/71) [1971] ECR 949 **18.4**

Beneditti v Munari (52/76) [1977] ECR 163 **19.3**

Beutzinger v Steinbruchs-Berufsgenossenscahft (73/72) [1973] ECR 283 **12.6**

Bozzone v Office de Securité Sociale d'Outre Mer (87/76) [1976] ECR 687 **12.6**

C

Caisse Primaire d'Assurance Maladie d'Eure et Loire v Tessier (neé Recq) (84/77) [1978] ECR 1 **12.6**

Campus Oil Ltd v Minister for Industry and Energy [1983] IR 82 **4.5**

Campus Oil Ltd v Minister for Industry and Energy (72/83) [1984] ECR 2727 **10.5**

Casati (203/80) [1981] ECR 1595 **14.4**

Coenen v Sociaal-Economische Raad (39/75) [1975] ECR 1547 **13.4**

Conegate Ltd v HM Customs and Excise (121/85) [1986] 1 CMLR 730 **10.5**

Coonan v Insurance Officier (110/79) [1980] ECR 1445 **12.6**

Consten SARL and Grundig Verkaufs v EEC Commission (56, 58/64) [1966] ECR 299 **10.3**

Costa v ENEL (6/64) [1964] ECR 315 **19.3**

D

Deryke (65/76) [1977] ECR 29 **17.4**

Denkavist v Anklagemyndigheden (21/78) [1978] ECR 2317 **17.4**

Deutsche Grammophon GmbH v Metro-SB-Grossmärket GmbH & Co KG (78/70) [1971] ECR 487 **10.3**

Donner v Netherlands (39/82) [1983] ECR 19 **10.3**

E

EC Commission v Denmark (171/78) [1980] ECR 447 **20.4**

EC Commission v Denmark (158/82) [1983] ECR 3573 **10.3**

EC Commission v Denmark (143/83) [1986] 1CMLR 44 **22.4**

EC Commission v France (167/73) [1974] ECR 359 **12.4**

EC Commission v France (168/78) [1980] ECR 347 **20.4**

EC Commission v Germany (12/74) [1975] ECR 181 **10.3**

EC Commission v Ireland (55/79) [1980] ECR **20.4**

EC Commission v Ireland (249/82) [1982] ECR 4005 **10.3**

EC Commission v Italy (7/68) [1968] ECR 423 **10.3, 10.5**

EC Commission v Italy (61/77) [1978] ECR 1279 **16.4**

EC Commission v Italy (169/78) [1980] ECR 385 **20.4**

EC Commission v Italy (43/80) [1980] ECR 3643 **3.14**

EC Commission v Italy (319/81) [1983] ECR 601 **20.5**

EC Commission v Luxembourg and Belgium (90, 91/63) [1964] ECR 625 **10.3**

EC Commission v Italy (170/78) [1980] ECR 417 **20.4**

EC Commission v UK (32/79) [1980] ECR 2403 **16.4**

EC Commission v UK (804/79) [1981] ECR 1045 **16.4**

EC Commission v UK (61/81) [1982] ECR 2601 **22.4**

EC Commission v UK (124/81) [1983] ECR 203 **10.3**

EC Commission v UK (165/82) [1983] ECR 3431 **22.4**

EC Commission v UK (40/82) [1984] ECR 283 **10.3, 10.5**

EC Commission v UK (261/85) (1988) IOECJ 3b/88 4.2.88 **4.3**

EEC Commission v Italy (7/61) [1961] ECR 317 **10.3**

EEC Commission v Italy (10/61) [1962] CMLR 187 **10.3**

Competition Decisions

GENERAL

1
BACKGROUND

TOWARDS THE TREATY OF ROME 1947 - 1957

1947   **UN Economic Commission for Europe**
Purpose : exchange of information on coal,
electricity and transport in Western Europe
Members : 28 countries
Marshall Plan
Purpose : economic relief provided by the United
States for the rebuilding of Europe

1948   **Organisation for European Economic Co-opera-
tion (OEEC)**
Purpose : first important move towards economic
co-operation in Europe
Members : 18 countries
Institutions : Council of Ministers, Executive
Committee, Secretariat
Benelux Union
Purpose : removal of customs barriers and closer
co-operation between Benelux countries

1949   **Council of Europe**
Purpose : greater economic and political co-oper-
ation
Members : now totalling 21 countries
Achievements : seen in the field of human rights
through the European Court of Human Rights
North Atlantic Treaty Organisation (NATO)
Purpose : military co-operation
Members : all Western European countries (except
Ireland, Sweden, Switzerland - France withdrew
from NATO but remains a party to the Treaty),
Canada and the USA

1950   **Schuman Plan**
Purpose : fusion of the coal and steel industries in
France and Germany and any other countries which
wished to participate under a single supra-national
body

1951	**Treaty of Paris** *Purpose* : establishing the European Coal and Steel Community (ECSC) *Signatories / member states* : Belgium, France, Germany, Italy, Luxembourg, Netherlands *Institutions* : supra-national in nature - High Authority, Consultative Committee, Council of Ministers, Assembly, Court of Justice
1952	**European Defence Treaty** *Purpose* : envisaging a European Defence Community (EDC)
1957	**Treaties of Rome** *Purpose* : establishment of the European Economic Community (EEC) and European Atomic Energy Community (EAEC / Euratom) *Signatories / member states* : Belgium, France, Germany, Italy, Luxembourg, Netherlands *Institutions* : supra-national in nature - Commission, Consultative Committee, Council of Ministers, Assembly, Court of Justice

TOWARDS EUROPEAN UNION 1957 - 1986

1959	**European Free Trade Association (EFTA)** *Purpose* : creation of a free trade area *Original members* : Austria, Denmark, Norway, Portugal, Sweden, Switzerland and the UK
1961	Irish application for membership of the EC (Lemass)
1965	**Treaty of Brussels ("Merger Treaty")** *Purpose* : institutional merger of the three Communities
1967	Irish application for membership of the EC (Lynch)
1970	Formal opening of negotiations for membership at Luxembourg
1972	Referendum on Irish accession to EC (amendment of Article 29 of the Constitution of Ireland)

1973	Accession of Denmark, Ireland and the United Kingdom (Treaty of Accession 22.1.72)
1976	**Tindemans Report** Discussion on the gradual development towards European Union with closer co-operation between member states as regards foreign policy; proposing regular meetings of the heads of governments, the strengthening of the role of the Council and a two-speed plan for economic integration
1979	First direct elections to the European Parliament **Report of the Three Wise Men** Discussion of the failure of the Communities in carrying out original and new policies
1981	Accession of Greece (Treaty of Accession 28.5.79)
1984	Second direct elections to the European Parliament **Draft Treaty establishing European Union (Spinelli Report)**
1985	**White Paper from the Commission to the Council** Details of unachieved Treaty objectives and laying down details for the achievement of those objectives by 31.12.92
1986	**Single European Act (SEA)** Accession of Spain and Portugal (Treaty of Accession 12.6.85)

2
AIMS AND OBJECTIVES

2.1 **The general aims and objectives in establishing a common market are to provide :**
- harmonious development of economic activities
- continuous and balanced expansion
- increased stability
- increased standards of living
- closer relationship between member states

[*See EEC Treaty, art 2*]

2.2 **The means of achieving those objectives :**
- elimination between member states on imports and exports of :
  - customs duties
  - quantitative restrictions
  - measures having equivalent effect to customs duties or quantitative restrictions
- establishment of a :
  - common customs tariff (CCT)
  - common commercial policy towards third countries
- abolition between member states of obstacles to free movement of :
  - persons
  - services
  - capital
- adoption of a common agricultural policy (CAP)
- adoption of a common transport policy
- institution of a system ensuring that competition in the common market is not distorted
- co-ordination of economic policies of member states
- approximation of the laws of member states to the extent required for the proper functioning of the common market
- creation of a European Social Fund
- establishment of a European Investment Bank (EIB)

- association with and promotion of trade and economic and social development of overseas countries and territories

[*See EEC Treaty, art 3*]

3
COMMUNITY LAW

DEFINITION
3.1 Community law cannot be defined within the accepted classifications of law
- Community law constitutes a "new legal order"
[*Case 26/62 : Van Gend en Loos v Nederlandse Administratie der Belastingen [1963] ECR 1 at p29*]

3.2 Community law consists of
- that part of international law governing treaties and international institutions
- EC Treaties and their Annexes
- secondary legislation generated by the Community institutions
- that part of national law implementing Community provisions

PRIMARY SOURCES OF EC LAW
3.3 The primary sources are
- the three Foundation Treaties (ECSC, EEC,Euratom), Annexes and Protocols
- Convention on Certain Institutions Common to the EC (1957)
- Merger Treaty (1965)
- Budgetary Treaties (1970, 1975)
- Treaties of Accession (1972, 1979, 1985) and Annexes
- Act of the Council concerning Direct Elections to the European Parliament (1976)
- Single European Act (SEA) (1986)

3.4 Duration of the Foundation Treaties
- The ECSC Treaty is of limited duration
  - 50 years
[*See ECSC Treaty, art 97*]
- The EEC and Euratom Treaties are of unlimited duration
[*See EEC Treaty, art 240; Euratom Treaty, art 208*]

- There is no provision for withdrawal, suspension or expulsion of member states but a negotiated withdrawal necessitating amendment of the Treaties is possible (eg the withdrawal of Greenland)

3.5 Scope and application
- The Treaties apply to both the land mass and territorial waters of member states and have certain extra-territorial effects
- Special status is granted to the GDR which is not regarded as a non-member state by the Federal Republic of Germany
- The Treaties do not apply to the Faroe Islands and to the British sovereign base on Cyprus
- Special provisions limiting the effects of the Treaties apply to : French Overseas Departments, Channel Islands, Isle of Man, Mount Athos, Canary Islands, Ceuta and Melilla

SECONDARY SOURCES OF EC LAW
3.6 Obligatory acts
- Obligatory acts are made by the EC Council or EC Commission in order to carry out their tasks in accordance with the Treaty

[*See EEC Treaty, art 189*]

- Obligatory acts take the form of (as a rule)
    - regulations
    - directives
    - decisions

3.7 Non-obligatory acts
- Non-obligatory acts take the form of (as a rule)
    - opinions
    - recommendations

3.8 Publication of secondary legislation
- Secondary legislation is published in the Official Journal of the European Communities

3.9   Terminology used by the Foundation Treaties when referring to secondary legislation

EEC TREATY	EURATOM TREATY	ECSC TREATY
regulations directives decisions opinions recommendations	regulations directives decisions opinions recommendations	decisions recommendations opinions

3.10   Regulations
[See EEC Treaty, arts 189-191; Euratom Treaty, arts 161-163]
- Regulations are general in scope and binding in their entirety needing no national implementation
[See EEC Treaty, art 189(2)]
- Defective legislation is presumed valid until declared invalid by the Court of Justice
- Regulations must be reasoned and based on Treaty provisions
[See EEC Treaty, art 190]
- Regulations must be published in the Official Journal
- They are binding on the date specified in the regulation or, in the absence of a commencement date, on the twentieth day after publication
[See EEC Treaty, art 191(1)]

3.11   Directives
[See EEC Treaty, arts 189-190; Euratom Treaty, arts 161-163]
- Directives are binding on each member state to which they are addressed as to the result to be achieved, the choice of method being left to the member states concerned
[See EEC Treaty, art 189(3)]
- Implementation must be complete and within a specified time limit
  - failure to implement a directive into national law will lead to enforcement proceedings
- Directives must be reasoned and must be based on

11

Treaty provisions
[*See EEC Treaty, art 190*]
- Although addressed to member states, directives may create rights on which individuals can rely
- Directives must be notified to addressees
     - directives are effective upon notification
[*See EEC Treaty, art 191 (2)*]

3.12 Decisions
[*See EEC Treaty, arts 189 - 190; Euratom Treaty, arts 161 - 163*]
- Decisions are binding in their entirety on those to whom they are addressed which may be member states, individuals or corporations
[*See EEC Treaty, art 190*]
- Decisions must be reasoned and based on Treaty provisions
[*See EEC Treaty, art 190*]
- Decisions must be notified to addressees
     - decisions are effective upon notification
[*See EEC Treaty, art 191 (2)*]

3.13 Recognising secondary legislation
- Each piece of legislation is given an official number by the Community
- *EEC and Euratom regulations*
     - unique number / year
  eg Commission Regulation (EEC) 189/89
- *ECSC decisions*
     - unique number / year
  eg Commission Decision (ECSC) 789/83
- *All other secondary legislation*
     - year / unique number
  eg Council Directive (EEC) 88/344

3.14 Approximation of laws
[*See EEC Treaty, arts 100-102, as amended by the Single European Act, arts 18, 19*]
- For the purpose of the proper functioning of the common market the laws of member states in certain fields must be "approximated"
[*See EEC Treaty, art 3(a)*]

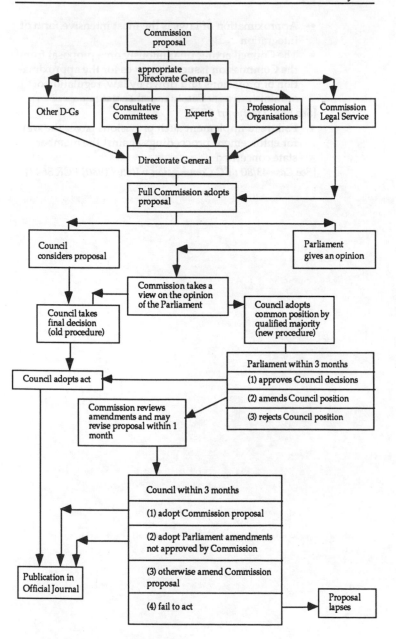

Fig. 1 : Legislative Processes

- Approximation of laws is the most intensive form of integration
- The Council acting unanimously on a proposal from the Commission issues directives for the approximation of provisions laid down by law, regulation or administrative action in member states

[*See EEC Treaty, art 100*]

- Failure to implement such provisions paves the way for enforcement proceedings against the member state concerned

[*See Case 43/80 : EC Commission v Italy [1980] ECR 3643*]

4
APPLICATION OF COMMUNITY LAW IN IRELAND

4.1 Ratification and incorporation into Irish law
- On ratification of the Treaty of Accession, Ireland acceded to the three Communities
- The European Communities Act 1972 gives force of law to the Treaty provisions which are intended to take direct effect in the member states

4.2 Implementation of secondary legislation
- *EEC, Euratom regulations, ECSC decisions are*
  - directly applicable in Ireland
  - automatically part of Irish law as soon as they are made
  - confer rights enforceable in the UK courts
- *EEC, Euratom directives, ECSC recommendations*
  - must be implemented in Ireland by statute or by subordinate legislation

  eg
  Sixth VAT Directive : Council Directive (EEC) 77/388 implemented by the Value Added Tax Act No. 22 of 1972
  Council Directive (EEC) 79/112 implemented by the European Communities (Labelling, Presentation and Advertising of Foodstuffs) Regulations 1982, SI 1982 No 205 and European Communities (Labelling, Presentation and Advertising of Foodstuffs) Regulations 1983, SI 1983 No 238

4.3 Enforcement of EC law
- *Directly*
  - through actions brought by other member states or Community institutions against Ireland for failure to fulfil its Treaty obligations

  [*See EEC Treaty, arts 169, 170; ECSC Treaty, arts 89, 88; Euratom Treaty, art 141*]

eg
> Case 61/77 EC Commission v Ireland [1978] ECR 417
> (fisheries)

- **Indirectly** : by references from national courts and
  tribunals for a preliminary ruling on points of EC
  law

[See EEC Treaty, art 177; ECSC Treaty, art 141; Euratom
Treaty, art 150]

eg
> Case 196/80 : Anglo Irish Meats v Minister for
> Agriculture [1981] ECR 2263 (interpretation of
> Commission Regulation (EEC) 1380/75 MCAs on
> beef and veal and interpretation of CCT

4.4   **Supremacy of EC law**
- In areas of conflict EC law is supreme over national
  law

4.5   **EC law before the Irish courts**
- There is general acceptance that EC law now forms
  part of Irish law

[See eg Campus Oil Ltd v Minister for Industry and Energy and
Others [1983] IR 82]

- **Treaty provisions**
  - only those provisions satisfying the conditions
    for direct effect are enforceable by the Irish courts
- **Secondary legislation**
  - it is recognised that regulations, directives and
    decisions confer rights and are therefore enforce-
    able in the Irish courts

THE INSTITUTIONS

5
THE EC COMMISSION

5.1 Composition and organisation

- A single Commission serves all three Communities
  [*See Merger Treaty, art 9*]
- There are 17 Commissioners
- The number of Commissioners may be altered by a unanimous decision of the Council of Ministers
- The EC Commission must include at least one but no more than two nationals of each state
  - the following member states have two Commissioners : France, Germany, Italy, Spain and the UK
  - the remaining member states have one Commissioner each

  [*See Merger Treaty, art 10*]
- The Commission has a President and six Vice-Presidents who hold office for renewable periods of 2 years

  [*See Merger Treaty, art 14; Act of Accession (1985), art 16*]
- The current President is Jacques Delors
- The current Vice-Presidents are Martin Bangemann, Sir Leon Brittan, Henning Christophersen, Manuel Marin, Frans Andriessen, and Filippo Pandolfi
- *Organisation*
  [*See Fig 2 on p22*]

5.2 Commissioners

- Commissioners are appointed by common accord of the governments of member states on the basis of general competence and independence from national interests
  [*See Merger Treaty, art 10*]
- Only nationals of member states may be members of the Commission
  [*See Merger Treaty, art 10*]
- Although Commissioners have to be appointed by agreement of member states' governments, each

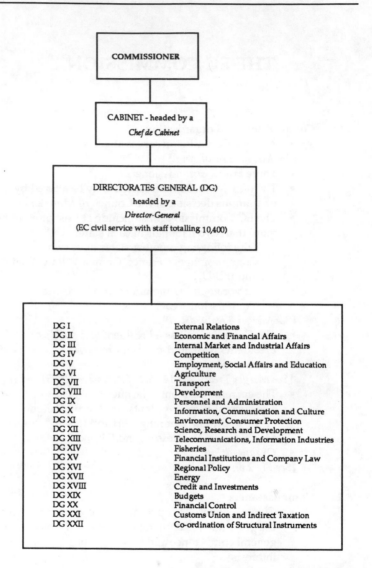

Fig. 2 : Structure of the EC Commission

country adopts its own criteria for selection
[*See Merger Treaty, art 11*]
- Commissioners are appointed for renewable periods of four years
[*See Merger Treaty, art 11*]
- Commissioners may resign or be compulsorily retired if they fail to fulfil the conditions required for the performance of their duties or are guilty of serious misconduct
[*See Merger Treaty, arts 12, 13*]
- Any vacancies must be filled for the remainder of the term unless the EC Council unanimously decides otherwise
- The Commission may be dismissed as a body by a motion of censure passed by the European Parliament
[*See ECSC Treaty, art 24; EEC Treaty, art 144; Euratom Treaty, art 114*]

5.3 Function and powers
[*See EEC Treaty, art 155; Euratom Treaty, art 124*]
- The functions and the powers of the EC Commission fall broadly into three categories :
  - guardian of the Treaties
  - initiator and guardian of Community policy
  - executive organ of government
- *Guardian of the Treaties*
  - the Commission must ensure that the Treaty provisions and measures taken by the institutions pursuant to them are applied
  - the Commission has the power to institute inquiries into alleged infringements of Community law by member states, corporations or individuals, to evaluate evidence and take appropriate measures
- *Policy initiator*
  - the Commission may formulate recommendations or deliver opinions on matters laid down by the Treaties

  eg *recommendations* - harmonisation of national laws
[*See EEC Treaty, art 102*]
  emergency action - balance of payments

21

[*See EEC Treaty, arts 108,109*]
> *opinions* - which are addressed to member
> states - capital movements

[*See EEC Treaty, art 72*]
> *failure to fulfil Treaty obligations*

[*See EEC Treaty, arts 169, 170*]

- *Legislative powers*
  - the Commission can make regulations, issue
    directives and take decisions

[*See ECSC Treaty, art 14; EEC Treaty, art 189; Euratom Treaty, art 161*]

- *Executive functions :*
  - the Commission's executive functions corre-
    spond to its duty to ensure that the Treaties are
    applied correctly

[*See EEC Treaty, arts 145, 155*]
  - certain executive powers vested in the EC
    Council are delegated to the Commission which
    cannot be delegated further

5.4 Procedure

[*See Provisional Rules of Procedure*]

- The Commission acts collectively by majority vote
- Regular weekly meetings are held

5.5 Location

- The Commission is located in Brussels

[*See Fact File, post, for Commission addresses*]

6
THE EC COUNCIL

6.1 Composition and organisation
- A single Council serves all three Communities
[*See Merger Treaty, art 1*]
- The EC Council is composed of representatives of each member state
[*See Merger Treaty, art 2*]
> - representatives should be members of the government of each member state
> - each member state may designate the appropriate minister for the relevant meeting of the Council

eg
General Council meetings are attended by the Ministers of Foreign Affairs
Specialist Council meetings by ministers responsible for the relevant portfolio, such as the minister for agriculture or transport
- The ministers, as delegates of their governments, are bound by precise instructions
- The Presidency of the Council rotates among the member states for terms of 6 months commencing on 1 January and 1 July

6.2 Functions and powers
- The Council exercises the powers and functions conferred upon it by each Treaty
[*See Merger Treaty, art 1*]
> - the jurisdiction conferred on the Council by the Merger Treaty is exercised according to the rules laid down in the Founding Treaties
[*See Merger Treaty, art 29*]
- The Council's main functions are :
> - to ensure the co-ordination of the general economic policies of the member states
> - to take decisions
> - to confer on the EC Commission, in the acts

which the Council adopts, powers for the
implementation of the rules which the Council
lays down
[*See EEC Treaty, art 145*]

6.3 Procedure
[*See Rules of Procedure*]
- The Council meets in private and regular meetings
  are held on the first Tuesday of every month
- The Council is convened at the request of the
  President, a member of the Council or the
  Commission
[*See Merger Treaty, art 5*]
- The President conducts the proceedings putting
  issues to the vote, signing and notifying the acts of
  the Council
[*See Merger Treaty, arts 2, 7, 9, 15*]
- *Voting*
  - any ministerial member of the Council may
  cast a vote on behalf of one other member state
  [*See ECSC Treaty, art 28; EEC Treaty, art 150; Euratom
  Treaty, art 120*]
  - normally voting is by a simple majority
  [*See EEC Treaty, art 148; Euratom Treaty, art 118*]
  - most of the Council's legislative powers have to

COUNTRY	VOTES
France	10
Germany	10
Italy	10
United Kingdom	10
Spain	8
Belgium	5
Greece	5
Netherlands	5
Portugal	5
Denmark	3
Ireland	3
Luxembourg	2

be exercised by qualified majority, for which a weighted voting system is used

6.4   The Secretariat of the Council and Committee of Permanent Representatives of Member States (COREPER)
- Continuity of the Council's work is provided by the General Secretariat and COREPER whose main task is the preparation of Council meetings
- *General Secretariat*
  - provides a permanent service to the rotating presidency, committees and working parties which carry out the day-to-day work of the Council
  - headed by a Secretary General appointed by the unanimous decision of the Council
  - divided into Directorates General, including a legal service
  - prepares the agenda, participates in the meetings of committees and working groups, liaises between the Council and the COREPER
- *COREPER*
  - set up under the Merger Treaty
  - main task is to prepare the work of the Council and execute the tasks assigned to it by the Council

  [See Merger Treaty, art 4]
  - consists of resident representatives of member states with ambassadorial rank
  - presidency rotates with that of the Council

6.5   The European Council
- Not to be confused with the EC Council, this can be seen as an extension to it
- The Council evolved from the regular summit meetings held between the government leaders/ heads of the member states
- It expresses itself through discussions in principle and broad political declarations

7
THE EUROPEAN PARLIAMENT

7.1 Composition and organisation

- The European Parliament (EP) consists of elected representatives from each member state

[*See EEC Treaty, art 137*]

- There are currently 518 members :

COUNTRY	MEMBERS
France	81
Germany	81
Italy	81
United Kingdom	81
Spain	60
Netherlands	25
Belgium	24
Greece	24
Portugal	24
Denmark	16
Ireland	15
Luxembourg	16

- The members (MEPs) are directly elected for a term of 5 years
  - elections were held in 1979, 1984, 1989
  - there are 4 constituencies in Ireland

Munster	5
Dublin	4
Connaught/Ulster	3
Leinster	3

- The European Parliament has organised itself as a
  political body
  - it is not purely a consultative body
  - members sit in multinational political groupings

PARTY	MEMBERS
Socialists	172
European People's Party (incl Fine Gael)	118
European Democrats	63
Communists	46
Liberals and Democratic Reformists	42
European Renewal and Democratic Alliance (incl Fianna Fail)	34
Rainbow Group	20
European Right	16

- *Administrative apparatus*
  - The administrative elements of the Parliament
    are the Bureau of the Parliament assisted by the
    Secretary General and a Secretariat
  - *The Bureau of the Parliament* consists of a
    President, 12 Vice-Presidents and 5 Questors
    elected for a term of two and a half years
  - *Questors* have a special responsibility for
    administrative and financial matters
  - *the Secretariat* looks after the organisational and
    administrative aspects of the Parliament
- The Parliament consists of 15 standing committees
  each specialising in a particular area of Community
  policy
  - the main function of the standing committees is
    to draw up reports forming the basis of debates

7.2   Functions and powers
- The Parliament's advisory and supervisory functions
  are exercised in 3 fields :
  - *Community legislation* through the consulta-
    tion and co-operation procedures
  - *political control* through the supervision of the

EC Commission and EC Council
- *budgetary control* through the preparation and
adoption of the Community budgets

7.3 Procedure

- *Sessions*
  - the Parliament must hold an annual
  session on the second Tuesday in March
  [*See ECSC Treaty, art 22; EEC Treaty, art 139; Euratom
  Treaty, art 109*]
  - it may meet in extraordinary session at the
  request of a majority of members, the EC Council
  or EC Commission
- *President and officers*
  - the Parliament elects its own President and
  officers from amongst its members and adopts its
  own rules of procedure
  [*See ECSC Treaty, arts 23, 25; EEC Treaty, arts 140, 142;
  Euratom Treaty, art 111*]
  - the current President is Lord Plumb
- *Voting*
  - resolutions are passed by absolute majority

7.4 Location

- Currently a source of contention within the
  Community, the Parliament holds its plenary
  sessions in Strasbourg but has offices and staff
  located in both Brussels and Luxembourg
  [*See Fact File, post, for Parliament addresses*]

8
THE EUROPEAN COURT OF JUSTICE (ECJ)

8.1 Introduction
- The role of the Court of Justice is to ensure that, in the interpretation and application of the EEC Treaty, the law is observed
  [*See ECSC Treaty, art 31; EEC Treaty, art 164; Euratom Treaty, art 136*]
- Cases may go before the Full Court , one of the six Chambers or the new Court of First Instance (as from September 1989)

8.2 Composition and organisation
[*See EEC Treaty, arts 165 - 168*] 15.
- The Court is composed of ~~thirteen~~ judges unanimously elected by the governments of the member states
- A President of the Court is appointed by the judges from among their own number and by absolute majority in a secret ballot
  - the office of President is for a three-year renewable term
- Presiding over the Chambers of the Court are four Presidents
  - they hold office for a one year renewable term
- The judges are assisted by six advocates-general
- Each judge and advocate-general is assisted by three legal secretaries who assist in drafting opinions and judgments
- The administration of the Court is under the control of the Registrar

8.3 Judges
- Judges are chosen from persons whose independence is beyond doubt and who possess the qualifications

required for appointment to the highest judicial
office in their respective countries

[*See EEC Treaty, art 167*]

- from 1973 to December 1974 the Irish judge was
Cearbhall O'Dalaigh
- from December 1974 to January 1985 the Irish
judge was Andreas O'Keeffe
- currently the Irish judge is Thomas F O'Higgins

- Office is tenable for six years and is renewable

8.4 Advocates-general

- Advocates-general are chosen from persons whose
independence is beyond doubt and who possess the
qualifications required for appointment to the
highest judicial office in their respective countries

[*See EEC Treaty, art 167*]

- the current UK advocate-general is Francis
Jacob QC
-from 1973 to October 1988 the UK advocate-
general was initially Jean-Pierre Warner who was
succeeded by Sir Gordon Slynn

- Office is tenable for six years and is renewable
- The office of advocate-general has no UK equivalent
but is similar to the Commissaire du Gouvernement
at the French Conseil d'Etat
- An advocate-general is required to consider the
issues in a case impartially and individually and to
reach his own personal conclusions as to what in law
should be done

- his "opinion" is then submitted to the Court
prior to judgment

8.5 Registrar

- The Registrar is elected by the judges by majority
vote after consultation with the advocates-general
- Office is tenable for six years and is renewable

8.6 Practice and procedure

- The Court sits in plenary session with a quorum of
seven judges
- The Court must sit in plenary session when hearing
cases brought by a member state or a Community
institution or preliminary rulings where the
Chambers do not have jurisdiction under the Rules

of Procedure

[*See ECSC Treaty, art 32; EEC Treaty, art 165; Euratom Treaty, art 137*]

- The Court may form Chambers to undertake preparatory inquiries or adjudicate particular categories of cases

[*See ECSC Treaty, art 32; EEC Treaty, art 165; Euratom Treaty, art 137*]

  - Chambers may have either three or five judges
  - there are currently six Chambers
  - Chambers adjudicate in staff cases and in so far as the case does not require the Court in plenary session to decide it
- Practice and procedure is based on the Rules of Procedure drawn up the Court
- *Stages in Court proceedings*
  - written stage
  - preparatory enquiry stage
  - oral stage

[*See Fig 3 on p36*]

- Parties must be legally represented at the oral stage
- *Languages of the Court*
  - the official languages of the Community :

Danish	Greek
Dutch	Italian
English	Portuguese
French	Spanish
German	

- *Judgments*
  - the Court usually follows the submissions of the advocate-general
  - in those cases where his submissions are not followed they can be considered as a dissenting opinion
  - only one judgment is given
  - judgments have binding force from the date of delivery
- *Enforcement of judgments*
  - if the Court upholds or declares invalid an act of a Community institution, that act may or may not be implemente,according to the decision of the Court
  - if the Court gives judgment against a member state under the ECSC Treaty, enforcement is

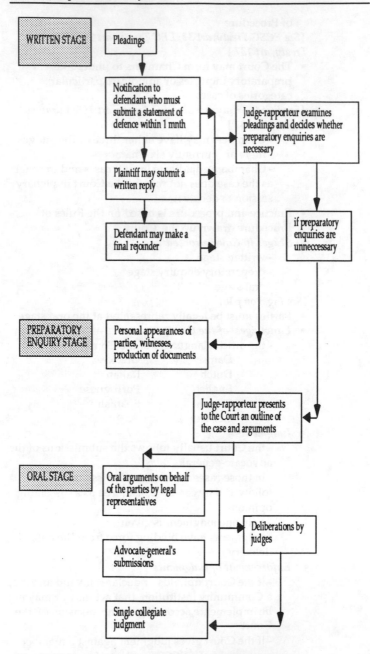

Fig. 3 : Procedural stages in the Court of Justice

through sanctions which may be imposed by the
EC Commission acting with the EC Council
- if the Court gives judgment against a corporate
body or individual in the form of a fine such
judgment debts are enforceable without further
formality
[See EEC Treaty, arts 187, 192]

8.7   Jurisdiction of the Court of Justice

* In actions where the EC Commission considers that a
  member state has failed to fulfil its obligations under
  the EEC Treaty
[See EEC Treaty, art 169]

* In actions where a member state considers that
  another member state has failed to fulfil its Treaty
  obligations
[See EEC Treaty, art 170]

* In actions brought by a member state, the EC
  Commission or EC Council or natural or legal
  persons as regards the legality of acts of the EC
  Council or EC Commission on the grounds of lack of
  competence, infringement of procedural
  requirements, misuse of powers etc
[See EEC Treaty, art 173]

* In actions brought by member states or other
  Community institutions where the EC Council or
  EC Commission, in infringement of Treaty
  obligations, have failed to act
[See EEC Treaty, art 175]

* In actions where the Court is asked to give a
  preliminary ruling concerning :
      - interpretation of the Treaty provisions
      - validity and interpretation of acts of
      Community institutions
[See EEC Treaty, art 177]

* In actions relating to compensation for damage
[See EEC Treaty, art 178]

* in actions between the Community institutions and
  staff
[See EEC Treaty, art 179]

* In actions relating to any arbitration clause contained
  in a contract concluded by or on behalf of the
  Community
[See EEC Treaty, art 181]

8.8 The Single European Act and the Court of First Instance

- The Single European Act laid down the legal foundations for the establishment of a Court of First Instance

[*See EEC Treaty, art 168a; Single European Act, art 11 ; Council Decision (ECSC, EEC, Euratom) 88/591*]

- It is expected that the Court will be operational from September 1989
- *Composition and organisation*
  - the Court is to have twelve members
  - *President of the Court of First Instance :* the members shall elect a President of the Court from among their number for a term of three years which is renewable
  - *Advocate-General :* the members of the Court of First Instance may be called upon to perform the task of an advocate-general
  - *Registrar :* the Court of First Instance shall appoint its own Registrar and lay down the rules governing his service
- *Practice and Procedure*
  - the Court of First Instance shall sit in chambers of three or five judges
  - the composition of the chambers and the assignment of cases to them shall be governed by the Rules of Procedure
  - in certain cases the Court of First Instance may sit in plenary session
- *Jurisdiction*

[*See Council Decision (ECSC, EEC, Euratom) 88/591, art 3*]

  - in disputes between the Communities and their servants

[*See EEC Treaty, art 179, Euratom Treaty, art 152*]

  - in actions brought by a member state or the EC Council as regards the legality of acts of the EC Commission on the grounds of lack of competence, infringement of procedural requirements, misuse of powers etc

[*See ECSC Treaty, arts 33, 35*]

  - in actions brought by a member state, the EC Commission or EC Council or natural or legal persons as regards the legality of acts of the EC Council or EC Commission on the grounds of lack of competence, infringement of procedural

requirements, misuse of powers etc
[*See EEC Treaty, art 173*]
- in actions brought by member states or other
Community institutions where the Council or
Commission, in infringement of Treaty
obligations, have failed to act in the
implementation of the competition rules
applicable to undertakings
[*See EEC Treaty, art 175*]
- in actions relating to compensation for damage
[*See EEC Treaty, art 178*]
- The jurisdiction of the Court of First Instance,
particularly in respect of actions brought under
the ECSC Treaty and those actions relating to
competition and anti-dumping proceedings, will
be reviewed after two years of operation of the
Court

8.9 Location :
- The seat of the Court of Justice and the Court of First
Instance is in Luxembourg
[*See Fact File, post, for Court of Justice address*]

9
OTHER INSTITUTIONS

9.1 Other Community institutions :
- Consultative bodies :
  - Consultative Committee of the ECSC
  - Economic and Social Committee
- Management and rule-making committees
- The Court of Auditors
- The European Investment Bank

THE POLICIES

10
FREE MOVEMENT OF GOODS

10.1 Introduction
- The EEC Treaty provides for the elimination of
  - customs duties
  - quantitative restrictions
  - charges having equivalent effect to customs duties
  - measures having equivalent effect to quantitative restrictions

10.2 Treaty provisions
- *EEC Treaty, art 3 (a)* : general legal basis of free movement of goods
- *EEC Treaty, arts 9 - 11* : general legal basis of free movement of goods
- *EEC Treaty, arts 12 - 17* : elimination of customs duties between member states
- *EEC Treaty, arts 18 - 29* : setting up of the common customs tariff
- *EEC Treaty, arts 20 - 37* : elimination of quantitative restrictions between member states and exceptions thereto

10.3 Principles and main cases
- The Treaty provisions are directly applicable
  - an importer in member state A is protected from national law imposing on products from member state B a duty higher than the Community rate or that imposed on similar national products

  [*See Case 26/62 : Van Gend en Loos v Nederlandse Administratie der Belastingen [1963] ECR 1*]
- The obligation to eliminate customs duties is absolute, exceptions being clear, unambiguous and strictly interpreted

  [*See Cases 52, 55/65 : Germany v EEC Commission [1966] ECR 159*]

- Restrictive import and export quotas are abolished
  [*See Case 7/61 : EEC Commission v Italy [1961] ECR 317*
  (suspension of the import of pork products into Italy);
  *Case 124/81 : EC Commission v United Kingdom [1983]
  ECR 203* (ban on French UHT milk products); *Case 40/82
  : EC Commission v United Kingdom [1984] ECR 283* (ban
  on French poultry)]
- An international agreement (with the exception of
  GATT) provides no defence to a breach of Commu-
  nity law
  [*See Case 10/61 : EEC Commission v Italy [1962] CMLR
  187*]
- Charges having equivalent effect to customs duties
  have been defined as
    " duties ... imposed unilaterally which apply
    specifically to a product imported by a member
    state but not to a similar national product and
    which by altering the price have the same effect
    on the free movement of goods as a customs
    duty"
  [*See Cases 2, 3/62 : EEC Commission v Luxembourg and
  Belgium [1962] ECR 425 at p 432 ; Cases 90, 91/63 : EEC
  Commission v Luxembourg and Belgium [1964] ECR 625*
  (import licences); *Case 7/68 : EC Commission v Italy [1968]
  ECR 423* (tax on export of art objects); *Case 158/82 : EC
  Commission v Denmark [1983] ECR 3573* (charges for
  health inspections)]
    - VAT is not a charge equivalent to customs
    duties
  [*See Case 39/82 : Donner v The Netherlands [1983] ECR 19*]
- Measures having equivalent effect to quantitative
  restrictions cover
    "all trading rules enacted by member states
    which are capable of hindering, directly or
    indirectly, actually or potentially, intra-
    Community trade"
  [*See Case 8/74 : Procureur du Roi v Dassonville [1974] ECR
  837; Case 272/80 : Frans-Nederlandse Maatschappij voor
  Biologische Producten [1981] ECR 3277* (inspection of
  imported goods); *Case 249/87 : EC Commission v Ireland
  [1982] ECR 4005* ("buy-Irish" advertising); *Case 12/74 : EC
  Commission v Germany [1975] ECR 181* (marketing); *Case
  120/78 : Rewe v Bundesmonopolverwaltung für Branntwein
  [1979] ECR 649* (alcoholic strength requirements)]

- Treaty provisions designed to remove such barriers on trade which are addressed to member states may also be relied upon by individuals protesting at national provisions restricting the free movement of goods within the Community
  [See Cases 56. 58/64 : Consten SARL and Grundig Verkaufs v EEC Commission [1966] ECR 299; Case 78/70 : Deutsche Grammophon GmbH v Metro-SB-Grossmärkte GmbH & Co KG [1971] ECR 487; Case 119/75 Terrapin v Terranova [1976] ECR 1039 (intellectual property)]

10.4 Exceptions

- There are certain exceptions to the basic principles which are outlined in the Treaty
- The exceptions are on the grounds of :
  - public morality, policy or security
  - protection of human or animal life and health
  - protection of national art, historic or archeological treasures
  - protection of industrial or commercial property
- The exceptions do not, however, constitute a means of arbitary discrimination or disguised restriction on trade
  [See EEC Treaty, art 36]

10.5 Examples of judicial decisions on the exceptions

- *Public morality*
  [See R v Henn, R v Darby [1978] 3 All ER 1190; Case 121/85 : Conegate Ltd v HM Customs and Excise [1986] 1 CMLR 739]
- *Public policy*
  [See Case 7/78 : R v Thompson [1978] ECR 2247]
- *Public security*
  [See R v Goldstein [1982] 2 All ER 53; Case 72/83 Campus Oil Ltd v Others v Minister for Industry and Energy and Others [1984] ECR 2727]
- *Health etc*
  [See Case 30/79 : Land of Berlin v Firma Wigei [1980] ECR 2071; Cases 141-143/81 : Holdijk [1982] ECR 1299; Case 40/82 : EC Commission v United Kingdom [1982] ECR 2793]
- *National heritage*
  [See Case 7/68 : EC Commission v Italy [1968] ECR 423]

11
CCT AND COMMERCIAL POLICY

11.1 Introduction
- Community external trade is based on :
  - Common Customs Tariff (CCT)
  - Commercial Policy

COMMON CUSTOMS TARIFF
11.2 Treaty provisions
- *EEC Treaty, arts 18-29*

11.3 Secondary legislation
- CCT was governed by *Council Regulations (EEC) 950/68, 97/69 (as amended)* until 1.1.88
- CCT has been replaced as from 1.1.88 by the Combined Nomenclature (CN) which is governed by *Council Regulation (EEC) 2658/87 (as amended)*

COMMERCIAL POLICY
11.4 Treaty provisions
- *EEC Treaty, arts 110 - 116*

11.5 Main principles
- Member states are to harmonise the systems whereby they grant aid for exports to third countries, ensuring, however, that competition is not distorted
  [*See EEC Treaty, art 112*]
- A common commercial policy is based on uniform principles relating to tariff rates, conclusion of tariff and trade agreements, export policies and the protection of trade in cases of dumping or subsidy
  [*See EEC Treaty, art 113*]

12
FREE MOVEMENT OF PERSONS

12.1 Introduction
- Freedom of movement of workers must be distinguished from the right of establishment enjoyed by self-employed persons [*see Ch 13*]; however, the latter cannot exist without the right to free movement within the Community

12.2 Treaty provisions
- *EEC Treaty, arts 48, 49* : general legal basis
- *EEC Treaty, art 50* : exchange of young workers
- *EEC Treaty, art 51* : legal basis for secondary legislation on social security

12.3 Secondary legislation
- *Council Regulation (EEC) 1612/68 (as amended)* : freedom of movement for workers within the Community
- *Council Directive (EEC) 73/148* : abolishing restrictions on movement and residence in relation to establishment and services
- *Council Regulation (EEC) 1408/71 (as amended)* : social security schemes for employed workers and their families moving within the Community
- *Council Regulation (EEC) 574/72 (as amended)* : procedural aspects of implementing 1408/71
- *Council Regulation (EEC) 2001/83* codifying/consolidating Council Regulations (EEC) 1408/71 and 574/72

FREE MOVEMENT OF WORKERS
12.4 Principles and main cases
- *The rights implied by the concept of freedom of movement*
  - right of entry

[*See Case 41/74 : Van Duyn v Home Office [1974] ECR 1337*]

> - right of residence

[*See Case 118/75 : Re Watson and Belmann [1976] ECR 1185*]

> - right to leave the host state
> - employment and free movement within the host state for this purpose

[*See Case 36/75 : Rutili v Ministère de l'Intérieur [1975] ECR 1219*]

> - right to remain in the host state on termination of employment within that state

• *Discrimination*

> - discrimination between workers on the basis of nationality as regards employment, remuneration and other working conditions is contary to EEC Treaty provisions and is to be abolished by all member states

[*See Case 167/73 : EC Commission v France [1974] ECR 359; and Ch 21 Social Policy*]

• *Application*

> - free movement of workers only applies to the citizens of member states
> - each state may define who are its citizens
> - free movement has been extended to cover refugees, dependants and spouses of Community citizens
> - free movement of workers does not apply to those employed in "public service"

[*See EEC Treaty, art 48 (4)*]

> - such a worker is protected, however, from discrimination on grounds of nationality

[*See Case 152/73 : Sotgiu v Deutsche Bundespost [1974] ECR 153*]

• *Definition* : the definition of "workers" includes :

> - persons in actual employment in the host state
> - persons looking for employment
> - unemployed persons who are capable of work and who have been previously employed
> - persons incapable of working through illness or injury sustained during employment in the host country
> - retired persons

- *Employment*
    - the term "employment" must be viewed in the sense of an activity which itself can be regarded as genuine work
  [*See R v Secchi [1975] 1 CMLR 383; Case 53/81 : Levin v Staatssecretaris van Justitie [1982] ECR 1035*]

12.5 Exceptions
- The free movement of workers may be restricted on grounds of :
    - public policy
    - public security
    - public health
  [*See EEC Treaty, arts 48(3), 56(1), 66*]
- Definition of "public policy" is still to be settled , ie whether member states can apply their own criteria or whether a Community policy has to be formulated
- Derogations are limited to extreme behaviour of the individual concerned
  [*See Case 131/79 : R v Secretary of State for Home Affairs, ex parte Santillo [1981] 2 All ER 897*]
- Any derogation from the Treaty provisions must be strictly interpreted
  [*See Case 41/74 : Van Duyn v Home Office [1974] ECR 1337; Case 36/75 : Rutili v Ministère de l'Inteéieur [1975] ECR 1219*]
- In the event of a derogation there must be a fair hearing
    - the procedure and rights of appeal must not be more onerous than that in comparable national cases
  [*See Case 98/79 : Pecastaing v Belgium [1980] ECR 691; Cases 115,116/81 : Adoui and Cornuaille v Belgium [1982] ECR 1665*]

SOCIAL SECURITY
12.6 Main principles and cases
- *Application*
    - there is no Community social security system
    - the objective of Community legislation is to co-ordinate national systems and provide protection for migrant workers and their families in the host countries

51

- social security rights are available to workers
and self-employed persons and their families
- students, although eligible for employment, are
not classified as "workers" for the purpose of
social security

[*See Case 66/77 : Kuyken v Rijksdienst voor Arbeidsvoorzien-
ing [1977] ECR 2311 (but see also Case 93/76 : Liègois v
ONPTS [1977] ECR 543 (post-graduate); Case 84/77 :
Caisse Primaire d'Assurance Maladie d'Eure et Loire v
Tessier (neé Recq) [1978] ECR 1 (au pair girls)]*

- a handicapped person who is incapable of
employment but who is a child of a worker may
be able to claim social security benefits

[*See Case 63/76 : Inzirillo v Caisse d'Allocations Familiales
de l'Arrondissement de Lyon [1976] ECR 2057]*

- **Classification of benefits**
  - *social security benefits* which are available as of
  right in consequence of affiliation to a national or
  private insurance scheme which are covered by
  Community provisions
  - *social welfare benefits* which are dependent on
  needs of the individual claimants and are
  awarded out of the public purse

- **Determination of beneficiaries**
  - beneficiaries are determined according to the
  systems of the host state
  - national legislation must be applied without
  discrimination on grounds of nationality

[*See Case 110/79 : Coonan v Insurance Officer [1980] ECR
1445]*

- **Benefits which can be claimed as of right in all
member states as "Community benefits"**
  - sickness and maternity benefits

[*See Council Regulation (EEC) 1408/71, arts 18-36 ; Case
1/78 : Kenny v Insurance Officer [1978] ECR 1489]*

- invalidity benefits

[*See Case 2/72 : Murin v Caisse Régionale d'Assurance
Maladie de Paris [1972] ECR 333]*

- old age pension

[*See Council Regulation (EEC) 1408/71, arts 44-51; Case
1/72 : Frilli v Belgian State [1972] ECR 457]*

- unemployment benefit

[*See Council Regulation (EEC) 1408/71, arts 67-71; Case*

126/77 : Frangiamore v Office National de l'Emploi [1978] ECR 725]
      - benefits for accidents at work etc
[*See Council Regulation (EEC) 1408/71, art 51 ; Case 173/78 : Villano v Nordwestliche Eisen-und Stahl-Berufsgenossenschaft [1979] ECR 1851]*
      - death grants
[*See Council Regulation (EEC) 1408/71, arts 64-66]*
      - family benefits
[*See Council Regulation (EEC) 1408/71, arts 72-79 ; Case 115/77 : Laumann v Landesversicherungsanstalt Rhein provinz [1978] ECR 805]*
• An employed person is subject to the law of his work place even if he resides in another member state
[*See Case 73/72 : Beutzinger v Steinbruchs - Berufsgenossenschaft [1973] ECR 283]*
• The same principle applies to self-employed persons
[*See Case 13/73 : Anciens ELS d'Angenieux v Hauenberg [1973] ECR 935]*
• Invalidity, old-age benefits, pensions etc acquired under the legislation of more than one member state are unaffected by the change of residence of the beneficiary
[*See Council Regulation (EEC) 1408/71, art 10 ; Case 87/76 : Bozzone v Office de Sécurité Sociale d'Outre Mer [1976] ECR 687]*
• *Aggregation and reimbursement of benefits*
      - *aggregation* requires the competent authority of the member state to take into consideration rights earned in another member state when computing certain benefits
      - *reimbursement* is where the paying state will recoup the payments made from the other state pro rata

13
RIGHT OF ESTABLISHMENT AND FREEDOM TO PROVIDE SERVICES

13.1 Introduction
- Freedom of movement of persons includes both self-employed and professional persons
- Services are for remuneration, in particular activities of a commercial nature
- The provision of such services is often linked to the exercise of a profession and in this the freedom to provide services is inseparable from the right of establishment
- Full enjoyment of the right of establishment how ever, is dependant on the recognition of professional qualifications

13.2 Treaty provisions
- *EEC Treaty, arts 52 - 58* : right of establishment
- *EEC Treaty, arts 59 - 66* : freedom to provide services

13.3 Secondary legislation
- *Council Directive (EEC) 89/48* : general system for the recognition of higher-education diplomas (enters into force in 1991)
- *Council recommendation (EEC) 89/49* : concerning nationals of member states who hold a diploma conferred in a third state

13.4 Main principles and cases
- *Application of right of establishment*
  - there is no definition of the group of people entitled to right of establishment
  - as distinct from "salaried workers", right of establishment applies to a group of people pursuing activities as self-employed persons or setting up and managing undertakings

[*See EEC Treaty, arts 52, 58*]

- *Discrimination*
    - the principle of non-discrimination on grounds of nationality has been strictly applied by the Court of Justice when considering establishment cases

[*See eg Case 2/74 : Reyners v Belgian State [1974] ECR 631* (Dutch lawyer's right to practise in Belgium); *Case 11/77 : Patrick v Ministère des Affaires Culturelles [1977] ECR 1199* (UK architect's right to practise in France)]

- *Residence qualifications*
    - a residential qualification of a properly qualified person is not a legitimate condition of his exercising a specific profession

[*See eg Case 33/74 : Van Binsbergen v Bestuur van de Bedrijfsvereniging voor de Metaalnijverheid [1974] ECR 1299* (lawyer); *Case 39/75 : Coenen v Sociaal-Economische Raad [1975] ECR 1547* (insurance agent); *Case 107/83 : Ordre des Avocats au Barreau de Paris v Klopp [1984] ECR 2971* (lawyer wishing to practise in both France and Germany)]

- *Amateur activities*
    - amateur activities are unaffected by Community rules

- *Harmonisation provisions governing the formation and exercise of certain professions*
    - medicine : *Council Directives (EEC) 75/362, 75/363, 75/364*
    - nursing : *Council Directives (EEC) 75/452, 75/453*
    - dentists : *Council Directive (EEC) 78/686, 78/687*
    - midwives : *Council Directives (EEC) 80/154, 80/155; Council Decisions (EEC) 80/156, 80/157*
    - vets : *Council Directives (EEC) 78/1026, 78/1027, 78/1028*
    - pharmacists : *Council Directive (EEC) 85/433*
    - general practitioners : *Council Directive (EEC) 86/457* (not yet in force)
    - architects : *Council Directive (EEC) 85/384*

[*For the position in respect of lawyers see 13.6, post*]

- The harmonisation process also covers other sectors such as agriculture, the film industry, mining, gas services, food and beverages, real estate etc

13.5 Recognition of higher national diplomas and qualifications

- The aim of the directive will be to ensure that professional qualifications issued in one member state are recognised in any other member state

  [*See Council Directive (EEC) 89/48, preamble*]

- All professionals whose qualifications fall within its scope will have a right to have their qualifications recognised in any other member state

  [*See Council Directive (EEC) 89/48, art 3*]

- Where the education/training is substantially the same between member states a professional's qualifications will be recognised

- Where the education/training is substantially different from that required by the profession in the host state there will be a choice between an aptitude test or a period of supervised practice not exceeding three years

  [*See Council Directive (EEC) 89/48, art 4*]

- Professionals will not be required to re-qualify or retrain in subjects they have already studied

13.6 The position of lawyers

- There are no harmonisation provisions governing the legal professions as yet

- Currently there are detailed provisions relating to the freedom to provide services by lawyers throughout the Community

  [*See Council Directive (EEC) 77/249*]

14
FREE MOVEMENT OF CAPITAL

14.1 Introduction
- In order for the economic freedom on which the EC is based to exist there must be liberalisation of financial operations

14.2 Treaty provisions
- *EEC Treaty, arts 67-73*

14.3 Secondary legislation
- *Council Directive of 11th May 1960* : implementing EEC Treaty, art 67 (now repealed by the 1988 provisions)
- *Council Directive (EEC) 88/361*

14.4 Principles and main cases
- Member states must abolish all restrictions on the movement of capital belonging to residents of member states

[*See EEC Treaty, art 67(1)*]
- *Discrimination*
    - discrimination based on nationality, residence of the parties or where the capital is invested is to be abolished by all states

[*See EEC Treaty, art 67 (1)*]
- Member states must liberalise their domestic rules governing the capital markets and credit sytems

[*See EEC Treaty, art 68 (2)*]
- *Balance of payments*
    - each member state is responsible for the standing of its currency and balance of payments, although exchange rates and member states' financial stability are matters for common concern
    - provisions exist for the co-ordination of member states' economic policies

[*See EEC Treaty, arts 104-105 and Ch 21*]

- *Main developments*
    - Monetary Committee to review the monetary
    and financial situation of member states (1958)
    - Economic Policy Committee (1974)
    - European Monetary System (EMS)

[*See below, 14.5*]

- *Currency restrictions*
    - member states still retain considerable control in
    respect of currency restrictions

[*See Case 203/80 : Casati [1981] ECR 2595; Cases 286/82, 26/83 : Luisi and Carbone v Ministero del Tesoro [1984] ECR 377*]

14.5 European Monetary System (EMS) and Exchange Rate Mechanism (ERM)

- The EMS came into existence on 12 March 1979
- *European Currency Unit (ECU)*
    - the Ecu is the central element of the EMS
    - the value is calculated as a basket of set
    amounts of EC currencies reflecting the relative
    gross national product of the member states
    - all currencies are included except those of Spain
    and Portugal
- *Exchange Rate Mechanism*
    - each member state which participates in the
    EMS exchange rate mechanism has a central rate
    against the Ecu which can be re-aligned
    - there are "floor" and "ceiling" rates between
    which the central banks are obliged to maintain
    the currencies
    - The UK, Greece, Spain and Portugal currently
    do not participate in this scheme, commonly
    known as the SNAKE

15
COMMON AGRICULTURAL POLICY
(CAP)

15.1 Introduction
- Agriculture is a sector which is closely linked with the European economy as a whole
- The rules governing agriculture derogate from the rules establishing the EC

[*See EEC Treaty, art 38 (2)*]

- The development of a common market for agricultural products must be accompanied by a common agricultural policy

[*See EEC Treaty, art 38 (4)*]

15.2 Treaty provisions
- *EEC Treaty, arts 38-47*

15.3 Secondary legislation
- For secondary legislation relating to individual agricultural markets *see 15.4*

15.4 Main principles
- *Objectives of the CAP*
    - increase agricultural productivity
    - ensure a fair standard of living
    - stabilise markets
    - provide certainty of supplies
    - ensure supplies to consumers at reasonable prices

[*See EEC Treaty, art 39 (1)*]

- To achieve the objectives the member states must adopt a common organisation of agricultural markets

[*See EEC Treaty, art 40 (2)*]

- *Common organisation of the markets*
    - undefined by the Treaty, but in practice takes the form of "European market organisation"

- involves the replacement of individual marketing arrangements for an agricultural product and introduces a Community-wide marketing structure for that product
- **Products affected by common organisation of the market include**
  -beef and veal

  [*See Council Regulation (EEC) 805/68, as amended*]
  - cereals

  [*See Council Regulation (EEC) 2727/75, as amended*]
  - dried fodder

  [*See Council Regulation (EEC) 1117/78, as amended*]
  - eggs and poultrymeat

  [*See Council Regulations (EEC) 2771/75, 2777/75, as amended*]
  - flax and hemp

  [*See Council Regulation (EEC) 1308/70, as amended*]
  - fruit and vegetables

  [*See Council Regulation (EEC) 1035/72, as amended*]
  - hops

  [*See Council Regulation (EEC) 1696/71, as amended*]
  - live trees etc

  [*See Council Regulation (EEC) 234/68*]
  - milk and milk products

  [*See Council Regulation (EEC) 804/68, as amended*]
  - oils and fats

  [*See Council Regulation (EEC) 136/66, as amended*]
  - pigmeat

  [*See Council Regulation (EEC) 2759/75, as amended*]
  - products processed from fruit and vegetables

  [*See CouncilRegulation (EEC) 516/77, as amended*]
  - raw tobacco

  [*See Council Regulation (EEC) 727/70, as amended*]
  - rice

  [*See Council Regulation (EEC) 1418/76, as amended*]
  - seeds

  [*See Council Regulation (EEC) 2358/71, as amended*]
  - sheepmeat and goatmeat

  [*See Council Regulation (EEC) 1837/80, as amended*]
  - sugar

  [*See Council Regulation (EEC) 1785/81, as amended*]
  - wine

  [*See Council Regulation (EEC) 822/87, as amended*]
- **Price system**
  - most Community markets are based on a common

price system within the Community and regulate
trade with third countries
- price systems comprise :
target prices
intervention prices
threshold prices
• *Structural reorganisation*
- modernisation of the farming industry
[*See Council Directive (EEC) 72/159, as amended*]
- assistance to farmers leaving the land
[*See Council Directive (EEC) 72/160, as amended*]
- professional training and advice
[*See Council Directive (EEC) 72/161, as amended*]
- dealing with problems of farming in less-favoured
areas
[*See Council Directive (EEC) 77/268, as amended*]
- co-ordination in relation to processing and
marketing
[*See Council Regulation (EEC) 355/77, as amended*]
- improvement in the efficiency of agricultural
structures
[*See Council Regulation (EEC) 797/85, as amended*]
• *Competition provisions*
- competition provisions (*EEC Treaty, arts 85, 86*)
only apply to production and trade in agricultural
products as determined by the EC Council
[*See EEC Treaty, art 42*]
• *State aids*
- provisions relating to state aids (*EEC Treaty, arts
92, 93*) may not apply

16
COMMON FISHERIES POLICY (CFP)

16.1 Introduction
- EEC Treaty provides for the basis of a common fisheries policy within the framework of the common agricultural policy
[See EEC Treaty, art 38 (1)]
- As recently as 1983 a set of provisions ultimately emerged relating to a separate common fisheries policy

16.2 Treaty provisions
- *EEC Treaty, art 38 (1)*

16.3 Secondary legislation
- *Council Regulation (EEC) 170/83* : Community system for conservation and management of fishery resources
- *Council Regulation (EEC) 171/83 as replaced by 3094/86* : technical measures for the conservation of fishery resources

NB : There are many provisions relating to individual types of fishery products, fishery vessels, nets etc and annual provisions relating to the total allowable catches (TACs) available to each member state

16.4 Main elements and cases
- *The main elements of the common fisheries policy*
  - equal access to fishery resources
  - structural reform
  - marketing organisation
  - conservation
- *The main cases*
  - *Cases 3, 4, 6/76 : Officier van Justitie v Kramer [1976] ECR 1279*
  - *Case 61/77 : EC Commission v Ireland [1978] ECR 417*
  - *Case 88/77 : Minister of Fisheries v Schonenberg [1978] ECR 473*
  - *Case 32/79 : EC Commission v UK [1980] ECR 2403*

- *Case 804/79 : EC Commision v UK [1981] ECR 1045*
- *Case 63/81 : R v Kirk [1984] ECR 2689*

17
TRANSPORT

17.1 Introduction
- An integrated transport policy is an indispensable element of the European Communities
- A common transport policy has developed piecemeal

17.2 Treaty provisions
- *EEC Treaty, art 3 (e)* : basic provision
- *EEC Treaty, arts 74-84*

17.3 Secondary legislation
- *Council Regulations (EEC) 141/62, 1002/67, 1017/68* : application of competition rules
- *Council Regulation (EEC) 3568/83* : tariff measures
- *Council Directive (EEC) 72/166* : insurance
- *Council Directive (EEC) 74/561, as amended* : freedom to provide services and right of establishment
- *Council Regulations (EEC) 543/69, 3820/85* : social provisions
- *Council Regulations (EEC) 1463/70, as amended, 3821/85* : recording equipment
- *Council Directive (EEC) 70/156, as amended* : type approval for motor vehicles and their trailers
- *Council Directives (EEC) 74/150, 79/694, as amended* : type-approval for wheeled agricultural and forestry tractors
- *Council Directives (EEC) 87/601, 87/602* : air fares and routes and passenger capacity

17.4 Main principles and cases
- *Application and scope*
  - common rules applicable to international transport to or from member states
  - conditions under which non-resident carriers may operate transport services
  - any other appropriate provisions

  [*See EEC Treaty, art 74*]

- the Treaty provisions refer only to transport by rail, road and inland waterway

[*See EEC Treaty, art 84*]

- the EC Council may extend this policy to air and sea

[*See Council Directives (EEC) 87/601, 87/602*]

- **Application of competition rules**
  - competition rules apply

[*See Council Regulations (EEC) 17/62, as amended, 141/62, 1002/67, 1017/68*]

- **Harmonisation and the implications of the EC Commission White Paper**
  - the Commission White Paper of 1985 details the failures in the field of transport policy and singles out the priorities for action

[*See Case 13/83 : European Parliament v EC Council [1986] 1 CMLR 138*]

- **Operational harmonisation**
  - *tariff measures* : bilateral agreements between member states relating to maximum and minimum charges,ie bracket tariffs applicable to rail, road and inland waterway transport

[*See Council Regulation (EEC) 3568/83*]

  - *non-tariff measures* : competition rules and conditions for the operation of transport services

- **Road transport provisions**
  - currently the most developed aspect of EC transport policy
  - *insurance provisions* relate to insurance against civil liability arising from the use of motor vehicles on the road

[*See Council Directive (EEC) 72/166, as amended*]

  - *transport operators* are subject to the provisions relating to the freedom to provide services and right of establishment

[*See EEC Treaty, arts 52-66; Council Directive (EEC) 74/561, as amended and Ch 13*]

  - member states may refuse an operator's licence to a person with a criminal record

[*See Case 21/78 : Denkavit v Anklagemyndigheden [1978] ECR 2327*]

  - *technical harmonisation* relates to standards of equipment, safety, comfort and control of pollution
  - *social harmonisation* relates to the establishment

of common standards of working conditions
[*See Council Regulations (EEC) 543/69, 3820/85*]
- standards apply to all drivers
[*See Case 65/76 : Re Deryke [1977] ECR 29*]
- member states are bound to ensure that the use of certain road transport vehicles is controlled by means of recording equipment
[*See Council Regulations (EEC) 1463/70, as amended, 3821/85*]
- As to the international implications see *Re ERTA [1971] ECR 263*

18
COMPETITION POLICY AND ANTI-DUMPING

COMPETITION

18.1 Introduction
- It is essential to the functioning of a common market that competition is not distorted

18.2 Treaty provisions
- *EEC Treaty, art 3 (f)* : basic provision
- *EEC Treaty, art 85* : agreements, decisions and concerted practices
- *EEC Treaty, art 86* : abuse of dominant position
- *EEC Treaty, art 89* : specific provision for state supported undertakings

18.3 Secondary legislation
- *Council Regulation (EEC) 17/62, as amended* : implementing EEC Treaty, arts 85, 86
- *Council Regulations (EEC) 141/62, 1002/67, 1017/68* : application of competition rules to transport
- *Council Regulation (EEC) 1983/83* : application of EEC Treaty, art 85(3) to categories of exclusive distribution agreements (block exemption)
- *Council Regulation (EEC) 1984/83* : application of EEC Treaty, art 85(3) to categories of exclusive purchasing agreements (block exemption)
- *Council Regulation (EEC) 2349/84* : application of EEC Treaty, art 85 (3) to categories of patent licensing agreements (block exemption)
- *Council Regulation (EEC) 123/85* : application of EEC Treaty, art 85 (3) to categories of motor vehicle distribution agreements (block exemption)
- *Council Regulation (EEC) 417/85* : application of EEC Treaty, art 85(3) to categories of specialisation agreements (block exemption)
- *Council Regulation (EEC) 418/85* : application of EEC Treaty, art 85(3) to categories of research and development agreements (block exemption)

- *Council Regulations (EEC) 3976/87, 2671/88, 2672/88, 2673/88* : application of EEC Treaty, art 85 (3) to agreements relating to air transport (block exemptions)
- *Council Regulation (EEC) 4087/88* : application of EEC Treaty, art 85(3) to categories of franchise agreements (block exemptions)
- *Council Regulation (EEC) 556/89* : application of EEC Treaty, art 85(3) to categories of know-how agreements (block exemption)

18.4   Main principles and cases

- *Agreements between undertakings*

    - all agreements between undertakings, decisions by associations of undertakings and concerted practices, which may affect trade between member states are prohibited

    [*See EEC Treaty, art 85 (1)*]

    - "undertaking" can include any company, or group of connected companies where a measure of control is exercised such as the parent / subsidiary relationship and is not limited by Community boundaries

    [*See Case 48/69 : ICI v EC Commission (Dyestuffs) [1972] ECR 557*]

    - all types of agreements, decisions and concerted practices may be covered by EEC Treaty, art 85, but not usually those between connected companies

    [*See Case 22/71 : Beguelin Import v G L Import Export [1971] ECR 949*]

    - certain agreements are expressly permitted by EEC Treaty, art 85 (3), and the Commission may recognise this either on a case-by-case basis, or via a block exemption

    [*See EEC Treaty, art 85 (3) and the provisions relating to block exemptions listed in 18.3 supra*]

    - a de minimus rule applies whereby agreements likely to have only a small impact will not be caught

    [*See EC Commission notice on agreements of minor importance OJ C231 12.9.86 p2*]

- *Abuse of dominant position*

    - any abuse by one or more undertakings of a dominant position within the common market or in a substantial part of it is prohibited as being

incompatible with the common market in so far
as it may affect trade between member states
[*See EEC Treaty, art 86*]
- "dominance" is not defined and may be
established with reference to :
the product market share
the geographical market share
the temporal market share
- dominance itself is not offensive but the unfair
exercise of dominance is - including takeovers
and mergers
[*See Case 6/72 : Europemballage Corpn and Continental Can
Co Inc v EC Commission [1973] ECR 2155*]
• *Scope and application of provisions*
- Community law applies only where trade
between member states may be affected; the test,
however, is extremely wide
[*See Case 56/65 : Société Technique Minière v Maschinenbau
Ulm [1966] ECR 235*]
- practices carried on outside the Community
may be penalised where their effect are felt
within the Community
[*See EC Commission Decision 85/202 - Wood Pulp*]
• *Enforcement of provisions*
- competition policy provisions are enforced by
the EC Commission, Directorate General IV
- the EC Commission has full powers to investigate alleged infringements of the Treaty
[*See Council Regulation (EEC) 17/62, arts 11-14; Case
136/79 : National Panasonic UK Ltd v EC Commission
[1980] ECR 2033*]
- the EC Commission has the following sanctions
at its disposal
fines - up to 10% of the annual worldwide
turnover of the undertaking penalised
periodic penalty payments
restitutive orders
- appeals to the Court of Justice are available
- for the practice and procedures involved see *Fig.*
4 on page 74

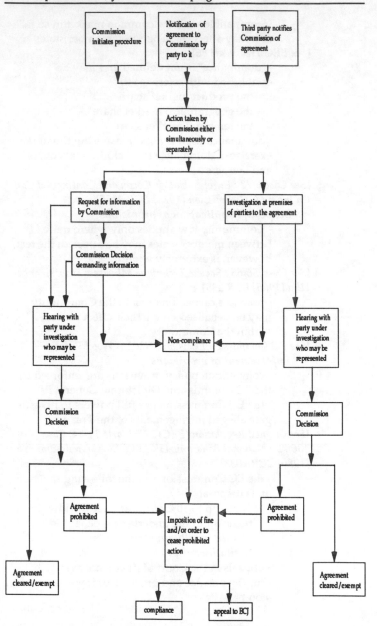

Fig. 4 EC Commission procedure in competition cases

ANTI-DUMPING

18.5 Introduction

- It is essential for the maintenance of fair competition within the Community that imports from non-member states having an unfair advantage over goods produced in member states are not permitted to enter the market

18.6 Treaty provisions

- *EEC Treaty, art 113* : basic provision

18.7 Secondary legislation

- *Council Regulation (EEC) 2423/88* : laying down measures for protection from dumped or subsidised imports not covered by the ECSC
- *Council Regulation (EEC) 2424/88* : laying down measures for protection from dumped or subsidised imports falling under the ECSC

18.8 Principles

- Dumping exists where the price charged for a product in the Community member state is lower than the price charged for that product in its domestic market of a non-member state
    - where a question of dumping of products is raised a reasonable sum to cover transportation costs should be included in the calculation of prices of such products within the Community
    - where a domestic price cannot be found it is for the Commission to evaluate the situation and construct a "price"
- It is for the EC Commission to implement anti-dumping policy
- Member states do not have the power to implement domestic rules independent of the Community
- Community anti-dumping rules must conform to those rules by the provisions of the General Agreement on Tariffs and Trade (GATT)
- *EC Commission sanctions*
    - the EC Commission will institute investigation proceedings and thereafter may impose provisional or definitive duties

19
STATE AIDS

19.1 Introduction
- National aids to industry distort the competitiveness within the European Community of undertakings

19.2 Treaty provisions
- *EEC Treaty, arts 92-94*

19.3 Main principles and cases
- It is incompatible with the common market for any aid to be granted by a member state which distorts or threatens to distort competition by favouring certain undertakings

[*See EEC Treaty, art 92 (1)*]
- *Definition of "aids"*
  - "aids" include :
    direct subsidies
    tax exemptions
    preferential interest rates
    favourable loan guarantees
    preferential terms of treatment as regards the acquisition of property and land
- Not all aids are prohibited :
  - prohibition only applies to selected undertakings and goods with the premise that such aids would affect trade between member states

[*See Case 730/79 : Philip Morris Holland BV v EC Commission [1980] ECR 2671; Joined Cases 296, 318/82 : Netherlands and Leeuwarder Papierwarenfabriek BV v EC Commission [1985] 3 CMLR 380*]
- *State aids which are compatible with the ideals of the common market*
  - have a social character granted to individual consumers

[*See Case 52/76 : Beneditti v Munari [1977] ECR 163*]
  - alleviate hardship resulting from natural disasters

77

- provide for certain regions of Germany to relieve hardship resulting from the division of the nation
- promote the development of regions afflicted by the low standards of living and high unemployment
- promote important European projects
- facilitate the development of certain economic activities

- *Powers of the EC Council and EC Commission*
  - the powers of the EC Council and EC Commission are defined
  - the procedures to be followed in cases concerning state aids are laid down

[*See EEC Treaty, arts 93, 94*]

- The relevant Treaty provisions are addressed to member states and do not create rights for individuals

[*See Case 6/64 : Costa v ENEL [1964] ECR 315*]

20
TAXATION

20.1 Introduction
- The EEC Treaty does not provide for uniform taxation throughout the Community

20.2 Treaty provisions
- *EEC Treaty, arts 95 - 99*

20.3 Secondary legislation
- The most important provisions relate to VAT [*See 20.5*]

20.4 Main principles and cases
- *The imposition of internal taxes on products from other member states*
  - taxes in excess of those imposed on similar domestic products are prohibited

  [*See EEC Treaty, art 95 (1)*]
  - this is directly enforceable

  [*See Case 57/65 : Lütticke GmbH v Hauptzollamt Saarlouis [1966] ECR 205; Case 55/79 : EC Commission v Ireland [1980] ECR 481*(import duties on foreign goods as regards Ireland)]
- *Internal taxation protecting domestic products*
  - such taxation is prohibited

  [*See EEC Treaty, art 95 (2); Cases 168/78 : EC Commission v France [1980] ECR 347; Case 169/78 : EC Commission v Italy [1980] ECR 385; Case 170/78 : EC Commission v UK [1980 ECR 417; Case 171/78 : EC Commission v Denmark [1980] ECR 447* (discriminatory indirect taxes on imported alcoholic beverages)]
- *Taxation on exports*
  - the principle of non-discrimination is applied by analogy to exports

  [*Case 51/74 : Van Hulst Zouen v Produktschap voor Siergewassen [1975] ECR 79*]

- *Single import tax*
    - the Treaty provisions simplify the multi-stage turnover tax by introducing a single tax on imports according to the product or group of products
  [*See EEC Treaty, art 97*]
    - these provisions are not directly enforceable
  [*See Case 28/67 : Molkerei-Zentrale Westfalen-Lippe GmbH v Hauptzollamt Paderborn [1968] ECR 143*]

20.5   **Main principles, provisions and cases relating to VAT**
- *Main provisions*
    - *Council Directive (EEC) 67/227 (First Directive)* : harmonisation of legislation relating to turnover taxes
    - *Council Directive (EEC) 67/228 (Second Directive)* : structure and method of application of VAT
    - *Council Directive (EEC) 69/463 (Third Directive)*
    - *Council Directive (EEC) 71/401 (Fourth Directive)*
    - *Council Directive (EEC) 72/250 (Fifth Directive)*
    - *Council Directive (EEC) 77/388 (Sixth Directive)* : replacing 67/227 and establishing a uniform basis of assessment
    - *Council Directive (EEC) 79/1072 (Eighth Directive)*
    - *Council Directive (EEC) 78/583 (Ninth Directive)*
    - *Council Directive (EEC) 84/386 (Tenth Directive)* : application of VAT to hiring out of moveable tangible property
    - *Council Directive (EEC) 80/368 (Eleventh Directive)*
    - *Council Directive (EEC) 86/560 (Thirteenth Directive)*
    - *Council Directive (EEC) 83/648 (Fifteenth Directive)*
    - *Council Directive (EEC) 85/362 (Seventeenth Directive)* : exemptions from VAT on temporary importation of goods other than means of transport
    - *Council Directive (EEC) 85/361 (Twentieth Directive)* : special aid granted to farmers as compensation for the dismantling of MCAs applying to certain agricultural products
- *Obligations of member states*
    - Member states are under an obligation to apply the principles contained in Community legislation
    - currently member states are free to determine the rates of tax but are not allowed to frustrate the operation of the Treaty taxation provisions

[*See Case 319/81 : EC Commission v Italy [1983] ECR 601*]
* *Scope and application*
    - the Community system applies to the supply of goods and services within Directive 77/388
    - VAT is chargeable within the territory of a member state to taxable persons
    - *"Taxable persons"* : persons or bodies carrying out independent economic activities
* *The EC Commission White Paper of 1985*
    - currently there is much discussion on the proposals raised by the EC Commission White Paper in particular as regards the lower and higher VAT rate   bands to be set and the abolition of "zero-rating"

21
ECONOMIC POLICY

21.1 Introduction
- Three areas make up Community economic policy
  - conjunctural policy
  - balance of payments
  - commercial policy

21.2 Treaty provisions
- *EEC Treaty, arts 101-103* : conjunctural policy
- *EEC Treaty, arts 104-109* : balance of payments
- *EEC Treaty, arts 110-116* : commercial policy

CONJUNCTURAL POLICY
21.3 Main principles and cases
- Member states should consult each other and the EC Commission in matters affecting economic trends
  - such matters should be regarded as of common concern

  [See EEC Treaty, art 103 (1)]
- In policy areas regulated by the Community, member states can no longer enact unilateral measures

  [See Re Galli [1975] ECR 47]
- Acting unanimously on a proposal from the Commission, the EC Council may decide on measures appropriate to meet the economic situation

  [See EEC Treaty, art 103 (2); Case 5/73 : Balkan Import-Export GmbH v Hauptzollamt Berlin-Packhof [1973] ECR 1091]
  - such powers are discretionary
  - the exercise of such powers is limited to those areas of Community concern

  [See Case 43/72 : Merkur-Außenhandels GmbH v EC Commission [1973] ECR 1055]

BALANCE OF PAYMENTS
21.4 Main principles

- A member state must pursue an economic policy which ensures the equilibrium of its balance of payments and confidence in its currency
  - at the same time that member state must take care to ensure a high level of employment and a degree of price stability

[See EEC Treaty, art 104]

- Member states are to co-ordinate their ecomic policies
  - the EC Commission recommends to the EC Council how such co-ordination is to be achieved

[Se e EEC Treaty, art 105]

  - in order to promote co-ordination of the monetary policies of member states, a Monetary Committee with advisory status was established
  - its tasks are to keep under review the monetary and financial situation of member states and to deliver opinons at the request of the EC Council or EC Commission

[See EEC Treaty, art 105(2)]

  - the Monetary Committee consists of representatives of governments and central banks of member states

- *Exchange rates*
  - member states may determine their own exchange rates with regard to the common Community interest and in line with Treaty provisions

[See EEC Treaty, art 107]

- *Balance of payments difficulties*
  - where a member state is in difficulties as regards its balance of payments the EC Commission is to investigate the position of the state concerned and shall recommend what measures that state should take to combat the situation
  - if such action taken by the member state fails to remedy the situation, the EC Commission, after consulting the Monetary Committee, may recommend to the EC Council the granting of financial assistance

[See EEC Treaty, art 108]

  - member states may take emergency protective measures when faced with sudden difficulties

[See EEC Treaty, art 109]

COMMERCIAL POLICY
21.5 **Main principles** [*See also Ch 11*]
- A common commercial policy if one of the fundamental principles of the Community

[*See EEC Treaty, art 3(b)*]
- *Scope and application*
  - export aids to third countries
  - customs agreements
  - commercial treaties

22
SOCIAL POLICY

22.1 Introduction
- Member states are to ensure the social as well as the economic progress of their countries by common action to eliminate the barriers which divide Europe
  [*See EEC Treaty, preamble, 2nd recital*]

22.2 Treaty provisions
- *EEC Treaty, arts 117-122* : basic provisions
- *EEC Treaty, arts 123-128* : European Social Fund

22.3 Secondary legislation
- *Commission Decision (EEC) 83/516* : European Social Fund
- *Council Directive (EEC) 75/117* : equal pay for men and women
- *Council Directive (EEC) 76/207* : equal treament as regards access to employment, vocational training and working conditions
- *Council Directive (EEC) 79/7* : equal treatment in the field of social security
- *Council Directive (EEC) 75/129* : collective redundancies
- *Council Directive (EEC) 77/187* : employees' rights on transfers of undertakings
- *Council Directive (EEC) 80/987* : protrection of employees on employer's insolvency
- *Council Directive (EEC) 63/266* : common vocational training policy
- *Council Regulation (EEC) 1408/71, as amended* : social security schemes for employed workers
- *Council Regulation (EEC) 574/72, as amended* : implementing 1408/71
- *Council Regulation (EEC) 2001/83* : codifying/consolidating 1408/71 and 574/72

22.4 Main principles and cases
- Member states are to promote improved working

conditions and an improved standard of living for workers

[See EEC Treaty, art 117]

- The social provisions contain no specific powers for the Community institutions to enact legislation; however, Treaty references to harmonisation and approximation of laws provide a legal basis for legislation in the social field
- The EC Commission has the task of promoting co-operation between member states in the social field, in particular relating to
  - employment, labour law and working conditions
  - basic and advanced vocational training
  - social security
  - health and safety
  - right of association and collective bargaining between employers and workers

[See EEC Treaty, art 118]

- *Equal pay and equal treatment for men and women*
  - member states should ensure the application of the principle that men and women should receive equal pay for equal work

[See EEC Treaty, art 119]

  - "pay" means basic or minimum wage oR salary
  - "equal pay without discrimination based on sex" means that pay for the same work at piece rates is calculated on the basis of the same unit of measurement, and that pay for work on a time basis is to be the same for the same job

[See EEC Treaty, art 119]

  - the EC Council has adopted directives in the following areas of equal treatment, the provisions of which muct be implemented in member states within a specified time :

[See Case 275/81 : Koks v Raad van Arbeid [1982] ECR 3013; Case 143/83 : EC Commission v Denmark [1986] 1 CMLR 44]

    pay

[See Council Directive (EEC) 75/117]

    treatment in access to employment , including promotion, vocational training and working conditions

[See Counicl Directive (EEC) 76/207]

    social security

[See Council Directive (EEC) 79/7]

men and women engaged in an activity in a self-employed capacity, and the protection of self-employed women during pregnancy and motherhood

[See Council Directive (EEC) 86/613]

occupational schemes

[See Council Directive (EEC) 86/378]

- references to the European Court of Justice

[See Case 129/79 : Macarthys Ltd v Smith [1980] ECR 1275; Case 69/80 : Worringham v Lloyds Bank [1981] ECR 767; Case 96/80 Jenkins v Kingsgate (Clothing Productsons) Ltd [1981] ECR 911; Case 12/81 Garland v British Railways Board [1982] ECR 359]

- infringement proceedings

[See Case 61/81 : EC Commission v UK [1982] ECR 2601; Case 165/82 EC Commission v UK [1983] ECR 3431]

• *Employment and working conditions*
  - the EC Council has adopted directives in the following areas :
    collective redundancies

[See Council Directive (EEC) 75/129]

  employees' rights on the transfers of undertakings

[See Council Directive (EEC) 77/187; Case 105/84 : Mikkelsen v Danmols Inventar A/S [1986] 1 CMLR 316 (meaning of "employee"); Case 135/83 : Abels v Bedrijfsvereniging voor de Metaalindustrie en de Electrotechnische Industrie [1987] 2 CMLR 406]

  protection of employees on employer's insolvency

[See Council Directive (EEC) 80/987, as amended]

• *Vocational training*
  - the EC Council, on a proposal from the EC Commission, must lay down general principles for implementing a common vocational training policy

[See EEC Treaty, art 128; Council Decision (EEC) 63/266]

  - to further the common vocational training policy the EC Council has adopted an action scheme for the mobility of university students (ERASMUS)

[See Council Decision (EEC) 87/327]

• *Social Security* [See Chapter 12]

- *European Social Fund*
  - the Fund was established to improve employment opportunities for workers in the EC and raise the standard of living

[See EEC Treaty, art 123]
  - the task of the European Social Fund is to assist in the implementation of policies aimed at equipping the workforce with requisite skills for stable employment

[See Council Decision (EEC) 83/516]
  - the Fund participates in financing operations concerning vocational training, guidance, recruitment, wage subsidies, resettlement and socio-vocational integration

23
REGIONAL POLICY

23.1 Introduction
- The Communities' concern for regional disparities is not only seen through its policies on state aids but also through the establishment of the European Regional Development Fund (ERDF) and Regional Policy Committee

23.2 Treaty provisions
- *EEC Treaty, art 235* : empowering the EC Council to take appropriate measures where necessary to attain Community objectives and where the Treaty has not provided other specific provisions

23.3 Secondary legislation
- *Council Regulation (EEC) 724/75, as amended and subsequently repealed* : establishing ERDF
- *Council Regulation (EEC) 1787/84* : reform of ERDF
- *Council Decision (EEC) 75/185* : establishment of Regional Policy Committee

23.4 Main principles
- *Purpose of ERDF*
  - the correction of the principal regional imbalances within the EC by participating in the development and structural adjustment of regions whose development is lagging behind
  - the conversion of declining industrial regions

  [*See Council Regulation (EEC) 1787/84, art 3*]
- *Scope of Community provisions*
  - co-ordination of policies

  [*See Council Regulation (EEC) 1787/84, arts 1, 2*]
  - creation of a single fund, the resources of which are allocated to member states by reference to parameters setting minimum and maximum assistance limits available to each member state

  [*See Council Regulation (EEC) 1787/84, art 4*]

　　　　- programme financing
[*See Council Regulation (EEC) 1787/84, arts 5-14*]
　　　　- project financing
[*See Council Regulation (EEC) 1787/84, arts 17-23*]
　　　　- studies
[*See Council Regulation (EEC) 1787/84, art 24*]
　　　　- simplified assistance rates
[*See Council Regulation (EEC) 1787/84, arts 25-31*]
　　　　- monitoring operations
[*See Council Regulation (EEC) 1787/84, arts 32, 33*]

- Allocation for the ERDF is determined annually in the Community budget
- The ERDF participates in the financing of Community programmes, national programmes of Community interest,' projects and studies
  - priority is given to certain investments in infrastructure, hill farming and farming in less-favoured areas
  - assistance from the ERDF must not distort competition
- *Regional Policy Committee*
  - *Purpose* : to contribute to the co-ordination of the regional policies of the member states
  - *Structure* : attached to the EC Commission and EC Council it comprises two members from each state and two members from the Commission; the European Investment Bank sends an observer
  - *Tasks* : to examine, at the request of the EC Commission or EC Council, or on its own initiative, problems relating to regional development, progress towards solutions and measures needed for further achievement of the Community's regional objectives

24
COMPANIES

24.1 Introduction
- In attaining a common market it is necessary for companies to be able to establish themselves and provide services in any member state
- The establishment formalities and structure of companies vary from state to state, thus creating barriers to trade

24.2 Treaty provisions
- *EEC Treaty, arts 54, 58* : right of establishment of companies in EC member states
- *Convention on the Mutual Recognition of Companies and Bodies Corporate*

24.3 Secondary legislation
- *First Council Directive (EEC) 68/151* : disclosure, obligations and nullity
- *Council Directive (EEC) 73/80* : capital duty
- *Second Council Directive (EEC) 77/91* : incorporation and capital
- *Council Directive (EEC) 77/187* : employees' rights on transfer of undertakings
- *Third Council Directive (EEC) 78/855* : mergers
- *Fourth Council Directive (EEC) 78/660* : annual accounts
- *Council Directives (EEC) 79/279, 80/390, 82/121* : stock exchange listings
- *Sixth Council Directive (EEC) 82/891* : division of companies
- *Seventh Council Directive (EEC) 83/349* : consolidated accounts
- *Eigth Council Directive (EEC) 84/253* : auditors and annual accounts
- *Council Directive (EEC) 85/611* : UCITS
- *Council Regulation (EEC) 2137/85* : European Economic Interest Groupings

24.4   Main principles

- On a proposal from the EC Commission, the EC
  Council must issue directives in order to implement
  the general programme for the abolition of existing
  restrictions on freedom of establishment, in particular
  co-ordinating the safeguards required by member states
  of companies or firms

[*See EEC Treaty, art 54 (1), (3)g*]

> - "companies or firms" means those constituted
> under civil or commercial law, including
> co-operative societies and other legal persons
> governed by public or private law, save for those
> which are non-profit making

[*See EEC Treaty, art 58*]

- The Council has adopted a number of directives
  relating to disclosure, incorporation, capital, mergers,
  accounts etc

[*see 24.3 ante; for current proposals see 28.4*]

- *The Draft Vredeling Directive*
  > - much discussed proposal relating to procedures
  > for informing and consulting employees of
  > undertakings with complex structures, in
  > particular transnational undertakings

- *European Economic Interest Groupings (EEIG)*
  > - *Purpose* : a new form of entity for use by
  > undertakings within the EC who wish to set up joint
  > ventures with each other
  > - *Task* : intended to encourage co-operation
  > between undertakings
  > - *Characteristics* : it has some characteristics of a
  > partnership and some of an unlimited company
  > - A group must not :
  >> exercise management powers over members
  >> hold shares in a member undertaking
  >> have more than 500 employees
  >> be a member of another grouping
  >> invite public investment
  > - *Registration* : member states must determine
  > whether groupings registered in their registries
  > have a legal personalit;, however, such a grouping
  > is not subject to the regulations and restrictions
  > imposed by national company laws

- *The European Company*
  > - efforts have been made for the establishment and

recognition of a European Company ("Societas Europae") which would be a company incorporated both under the laws of the member states and EC law

25
FINANCIAL SERVICES

25.1 Introduction
- In relation to the field of financial services, ie banking, financial and credit institutions, stock exchanges and the business of insurance, Community activity centres on the right of establishment and freedom to provide services

25.2 Treaty provisions
- *EEC Treaty, arts 52-66* : right of establishment and freedom to provide services
[*See Chapters 13, 14*]

BANKING AND FINANCIAL INSTITUTIONS
25.3 Secondary legislation
- *Council Directive (EEC) 73/183* : abolition of restrictions on freedom of establishment
- *Council Directive (EEC) 86/653* : annual accounts

25.4 Main principles
- Member states have an obligation to abolish restrictions impeding the right of establishment and freedom to provide services by banks and other financial institutions
[*See Council Directive (EEC) 73/183*]
- Institutions and persons falling within these provisions are :
  - banks
  - savings and loan undertakings
  - underwriting, surety and guarantee syndicates
  - brokers
  - intermediaries
  - foreign exchange offices, stock exchanges, metal markets, clearing houses
- Those benefiting from the abolition of restrictions may join professional or trade organisations under the same

condittions as nationals of the host state
[*See Council Directive (EEC) 73/183, arts 4, 5*]
- Member states may require unestablished foreign
  undertakings to be registered on a special list before
  they can provide banking services
[*See Council Directive (EEC) 73/183, art 6*]

CREDIT INSTITUTIONS
25.5   Secondary legislation
- *Council Directive (EEC) 77/780 , as amended*:
  co-ordination of national provisions
- *Council Directive (EEC) 83/350* : supervision
- *Council Directive (EEC) 89/117* : branch accounts

25.6   Main provisions
- *Definition*
  - an undertaking whose business is to receive
    deposits or other repayable funds from the public
    and to grant credits for its own accounts
[*See Council Directive (EEC) 77/780, art 1, as amended*]
  - central banks, post office giro institutions and
    certain specified institutions are excluded
[*See Council Directive (EEC) 77/780, art 2*]
- Credit institutions may carry on business as such if they
  are authorised by the member states in which they are
  established
- Member states are to ensure that all employees of
  national authorities in charge of supervising credit
  institutions are bound by professional secrecy
[*See Council Directive (EEC) 77/780, art 12; Case 110/84 :*
Gemeente Hillegom v Hillenius (1986) Times 2 January]
- Member states may lay down certain requirements for
  obtaining authorisation to carry on the business of a
  credit institution
[*See Council Directive (EEC) 77/780,, art 3*]
  - authorisation may be withdrawn by a competent
    authority where irregularities have occurred, the
    institution in question no longer possesses
    sufficient funds or fulfils the conditions under which
    the authority was granted or fails to make use of the
    authority within twelve months
[*See Council Directive (EEC) 77/780, art 8*]

STOCK EXCHANGES
25.7   Secondary legislation
- *Council Directive (EEC) 79/279* : admission
- *Council Directive (EEC) 80/390* : listing particulars

25.8   Main principles
- *Application of provisions*
    - Community provisions apply to securities in general, including those issued by third countries and international public bodies
- Each member state designates the national authority competent to decide on the admission of securities to official listing on the stock exchange
- Securities may not be admitted unless the conditions laid down by Community law are satisfied
    - admission to listing is subject to adherence to certain conditions

[*See Council Directive (EEC) 79/279, art 4; Council Directive (EEC) 80/390, art 3*]

- Competent authorities of member states are to co-operate with each other and exchange information

[*See Council Directive (EEC) 79/279, art 18*]

- *Contact Committee* : established to facilitate
    - harmonised implementation of directives
    - establishment of concerted attitudes between member states on additional or more stringent requirements for the admission of securities
    - consultation on supplements to improve listing particulars
    - advise the EC Commission on amendments to Community legislation

INSURANCE
25.9   Secondary legislation
- *Council Directive (EEC) 64/225* : reinsurance
- *Council Directive (EEC) 72/166, as amended* : motor insurance
- *Council Directive (EEC) 77/92* : insurance agents and brokers
- *Council Directive (EEC) 78/473* : co-insurance
- *Council Directives (EEC) 87/344, 88/357* : direct non-life insurance
- *Council Directive (EEC) 79/267* : direct life assurance

25. 10 Main principles

- "Insurance" is not generally defined by Community legislation but covers a variety of activities varying from accident to life assurance
- The following areas are affected by Community legislation
  - direct life assurance
  - direct non-life insurance
  - reinsurance
  - co-insurance
  - right of establishment and freedom to provide services of insurance agents and brokers
  - motor insurance

[*See 28.9, ante, for relevant provisions*]

- Within each specific insurance field there are provisions on
  - proof of no previous bankruptcy and good repute
  - distinctive rules as to Community and non-Community undertakings
  - admission to business of Community undertakings
  - conditions for carrying on business of an undertaking
  - withdrawal of authorisation

26
ENVIRONMENTAL POLICY

26.1 Introduction
- Prior to the Single European Act a series of action programmes relating to the environment were introduced, under which numerous directives have been adopted

26.2 Treaty provisions
- *EEC Treaty, arts 130r-130t, as added by the Single European Act*

26.3 Secondary legislation
- See individual action areas listed in 26.4, post

26.4 Main principles
- *Objects of Community action*
    - preservation, protection and improvement of the quality of the environment
    - contribution towards protecting human health
    - ensuring prudent and rational use of natural resources

  [*See EEC Treaty, art 130r (1)*]
- When taking action the following are to be considered
    - available scientific and technical data
    - regional environmental conditions
    - cost and benefits of action
    - economic and social development of the EC as a whole

  [*See EEC Treaty, art 130r (3)*]
- The EC Council acting unanimously on a proposal from the EC Commission and after consultation with the European Parliament and the Economic and Social Committee shall decide what action should be taken

  [*See EEC Treaty, art 130s*]
    - protective measures adopted by the EC do not prevent member states from introducing more

stringent measures
[*See EEC Treaty, art 130t*]
• Measures have been taken in relation to
   - air pollution
      gaseous pollutants
[*See Council Directives (EEC) 70/220, as amended, 73/306, 75/716, 76/156, as amended, , 77/537, 83/351; Commission Directives `77/102, 78/665*]
      lead
[*See Council Directives (EEC) 77/312, 78/611, 82/884, 85/210, 88/609*]
         industrial plants and large combination plants
[*See Council Directives (EEC) 75/441, 80/779, as amended, 84/360, 85/203, as amended; Council Decision (EEC) 81/462; Commission Regulation (EEC) 3528/86*]
      exhaust systems
[*See Council Directives (EEC) 70/157, as amended, 74/150, 78/1015, 86/594*]
      construction plants
[*See Council Directive (EEC) 79/113, as amended*]
      aircraft
[*See Council Directive (EEC) 80/51*]
   - water
      detergents
[*See Council Directives (EEC) 73/404, 73/405, as amended*]
      sewage
[*See Council Directives (EEC) 77/651, 79/311; Council Decision (EEC) 76/160*]
         surface and fresh water
[*See Council   Directives (EEC) 75/440, 79/869, 80/778: Convention for the Protection of the Rhine*]
         territorial waters
[*See Council Directive (EEC) 76/464; Convention for Prevention of Marine Pollution*]
      sea water
[*See Council Directives (EEC) 76/464, 82/176, 83/513; Convention for Prevention of Marine Pollution; Convention for the Protection of the Mediterranean Sea against Pollution*]
   - land pollution
      waste disposal
[*See Council Directive (EEC) 75/442*]
      waste oils
[*See Council Directive (EEC) 75/439*]

toxic waste
[*See Council Directives (EEC) 78/319, 84/631*]
- radiation and storage of radioactive waste
- conservation
wild birds
[*See Council Directive (EEC) 79/409*]
wildlife and natural habitats
[*See Council Directive (EEC) 82/72*]
wild animals
[*See Council Directive (EEC) 82/461*]
trade in endangered species
[*See Council Regulation (EEC) 3626/82*]
- public protection
major accident hazards
[*See Council Directive (EEC) 82/501*]

27
CONSUMERS

27.1 Introduction
- As with environmental policy a series of action programmes have been initiated in relation to consumer protection and information policy
- The Community has taken action in the following areas
  - protection of consumers' health and safety
  - consumer information
  - protection of consumers' economic interest

27.2 Secondary legislation
- See individual action areas listed in 27.3, post

27.3 Protection of consumers' health and safety
- *Foodstuffs*
  - additives

  [*See Council Directive (EEC) 89/107*]
  - antioxidants

  [*See Council Directive (EEC) 70/357, as amended*]
  - citrus fruit

  [*See Council Directive (EEC) 67/472*]
  - cocoa and chocolate products

  [*See Council Directive (EEC) 73/241, as amended*]
  - coffee

  [*See Council Directive (EEC) 77/436*]
  - colouring matters

  [*See Council Directive of 23 October 1962, as amended*]
  - dietetic foods

  [*See Council Directive (EEC) 77/94*]
  - emulsifiers, stabilisers, thickeners and gelling agents

  [*See Council Directive (EEC) 74/329, as amended*]
  - fruit juices

  [*See Council Directive (EEC) 75/726*]
  - honey

  [*See Council Directive (EEC) 74/409*]
  - jams and jellies

  [*See Council Directive (EEC) 79/693, as amended*]

- milk

[*See Council Directive (EEC) 76/118*]
- mineral waters

[*See Council Directive (EEC) 80/777, as amended*]
- preservatives

[*See Council Directive (EEC) 64/54, as amended*]
- sampling and analysis

[*See Council Directives (EEC) 85/358, 85/591*]
- sugar

[*See Council Directive (EEC) 73/437*]
- **Consumer durables**

[*See Council Directives (EEC) 69/493, 73/360, 76/764*]
- **Cosmetics**

[*See Council Directive (EEC) 76/768*]
- **Dangerous substances**
    - aerosol dispensers

[*See Council Directive (EEC) 75/324*]
    - classification, packaging and labelling

[*See Council Directive (EEC) 67/548, 73/173*]
    - electrical equipment

[*See Council Directive (EEC) 73/23*]
    - liability for defective products

[*See Council Directive (EEC) 85/374; Council Regulation (EEC) 3842/86*]
    - marketing and use

[*See Council Directive (EEC) 76/769*]
- **Detergents**

[*See Council Directive (EEC) 73/404*]
- **Fertilisers, pesticides etc**
    - fertilisers

[*See Council Directive (EEC) 76/116*]
    - pesticide residues

[*See Council Directive (EEC) 76/895*]
    - plant protective products

[*See Council Directive (EEC) 79/117*]
- **Materials and articles in contact with foodstuffs**

[*See Council Directives (EEC) 76/893, 83/229, 89/109*]
- **Medicinal products**

[*See Council Directives (EEC) 65/65, 78/25, 89/105; Case 35/85 Procureur de la Republique v Tissier [1987] 1 CMLR 551 (definition)*]
- **Motor vehicles**
    - provisions range from type approval, steering

equipment, recording equipment to seat belts etc
[*See Ch 17*]
* *Toys*
[*See Council Directive (EEC) 76/769*]
* *Veterinary products*
    - bovine animals and swine
[*See Council Directive (EEC) 64/432*]
    - feedingstuffs
[*See Council Directive (EEC) 70/373* (sampling), *70/524*
(additives), *74/63, 87/153* (additives)]
    - fresh meat
[*See Council Directive (EEC) 64/433*]
    - poultrymeat
[*See Council Directive (EEC) 71/118*]

27.4   **Consumer information**
* *Labelling*
[*See Council Directives (EEC) 67/548, 79/112*]
* *Measurements*
* *Packaging*
[*See Council Directives (EEC) 71/316, 75/106, 75/107, 76/211*]
* *Pricing of foodstuffs*
[*See Council Directive (EEC) 79/581*]

27.5   **Protection of consumers' economic interest**
* *Consumer credit agreements*
[*See Council Directive (EEC) 87/102*]
* *Doorstep selling*
[*See Council Directive (EEC) 85/577*]
* *Misleading advertising*
[*See Council Directive (EEC) 84/450*]

28
THE WAY FORWARD

28.1 Introduction
- In recent years there has been a noticeable increase in Community legislative activity in areas other than those relating purely to the Treaty-based policies
- An added impetus to Community activities was given by the EC Commission White Paper of 1985 on the completion of the internal market and by the Single European Act

28.2 Exploding the myth of "1992"
- The EEC Treaty contained fundamental provisions which were aimed at abolishing the existing barriers between Community member states
- The Community has been slowly moving and working towards a single European market since 1957
- The Single European Act commits the EC member states to the aim of progressively establishing a single market by 31 December 1992
  - a single market is an area without internal frontiers in which the free movement of goods, persons, services and capital is ensured
  - the single market envisaged by the EEC Treaty has now been extended by the Single European Act
- The accelerated progress towards the creation of a single market took its starting point from the 1985 White Paper which outlined the specific measures necessary to remove the remaining obstacles to trade etc by 1993
  - 300 measures were proposed, these have now been reduced to 279, some 200 of which have been approved and 100 enacted by means of secondary legislation
  - priorities are identified under the following headings
    - removal of physical barriers
    - removal of technical barriers
    - removal of fiscal barriers

SOME ASPECTS OF DEVELOPMENTS
AFFECTING YOU

28.3 **Broadcasting**
- Broadcasting by satellite
- Draft Convention on Trans-Frontier Broadcasting
- Draft EC Directive on broadcasting relating to
  - contents of programmes
  - advertising
  - copyright

[*See Com (88) 154 final OJ C110 27.4.88 p3*]
- EC Commission Green Paper on Copyright

[*See Com (88) 172 final*]
- High Definition Television (HDTV)

[*See Com (88) 659 final OJ C37 14.2.89 p5*]

28.4 **Company law**
- Company structure
  - boards of plcs
  - worker participation
  - AGMs
- Group of companies with a plc as a subsidiary
- Mergers between plcs registered in different member states
- Company accounts
- Takeovers

[*See Draft Thirteenth Company Law Directive - Com (88) 823 OJ C64 14.3.89 p8*]
- Mergers and acquisitions

[*See Com (88) 97 final OJ C130 19.5.88 p4*]
- European Company Statute

28.5 **Competition**
- Merger control

[*See Com (88) 97 final OJ C130 19.5.88 p4*]
- More stringent control of state aids

28.6 **Consumers**
- Package travel

[*See Com (88) 41 final*]
- Rights and liabilities relating to electronic payment cards

28.7 **Environment**
- Permissible noise levels

- Protection of the ozone layer
- Emissions from motor vehicles

28.8 External Relations
- New round of GATT negotiations
- Closer relationship with EFTA member states
- Possible applications for membership of the EC from Austria and Norway

28.9 Financial Services
- *Banking*
  - single banking licence
  [*See Draft Second Banking Directive (EEC) Com (87) 715 final OJ C84 31.3.88 p1*]
  - home country control
  [*See Draft Second Banking Directive (EEC) Com (87) 715 final OJ C84 31.3.88 p1*]
  - mutual recognition
  [*See Draft Second Banking Directive (EEC) Com (87) 715 final OJ C84 31.3.88 p1*]
  - own funds
  [*See Com (88) 15 final OJ C32 5.2.88 p2*]
  - solvency ratios
  [*See Com (88) 194) final OJ C135 25.5.88 p4*]
  - reorganisation, winding-up and deposit guarantee schemes
  [*See Com (88) 4 final OJ C36 8.2.88 p1*]
  - mortgage credit
  - electronic payment systems
- *Securities*
  - investment services
  [*See Com (88) 778 OJ C43 22.2.89 p7*]
  - disclosure of information
  - insider trading
- *Life / Non-life insurance*
  - winding-up of insurance companies
  - motor insurance
  - terms and conditions of insurance contracts
  - freedom to provide services
- *Capital movements*
  - co-ordination of member states' fiscal policies
  - protection of investors

28.10 Food and drugs
- *Food*
  - foods for particular nutritional uses
  - additives

  [*See Council Directive (EEC) 89/107*]
  - materials and articles in contact with food

  [*See Council Directive (EEC) 89/109*]
  - food labelling
  - inspection of foodstuffs
  - quick frozen foods

  [*See Council Directive (EEC) 89/108*]
  - irradiation and its effects on foods
  - batch marking
- *Medicines*
  - licensing
  - marketing
  - pricing

  [*See Council Directive (EEC) 89/105*]

28.11 Free Movement of Goods within the EC
- Abolition of duties
- Other fiscal arrangements
- Statistics on visible trade
- Rules relating to drugs and firearms

28.12 Free Movement of Persons
- Immigration rules

28.13 Health and Safety
- Increased protection for workers
- EC obligation to market safe products

28.14 Information Technology
- Action plan for the development of an information services market

  [*See Council Directive (EEC) 88/524*]
- Common standards for equipment

28.15 Intellectual Property
- Community Patent

  [*See European Patent Convention (Council of Europe), Community Patent Convention (1975 - not yet in force)*]
- Community Trademark

  [*See Council Directive (EEC) 89/104*]

- Copyright
  - commercial counterfeiting
  - home recording and video taping
  - video rental rights
  - computer programmes

  [*See EC Commission Green Paper on Copyright Com (88) 172 final*]

- Legal protection of biotechnological inventions

  [*See Com (88) 496 final OJ C10 13.1.89 p3*]

28.16 Right of establishment and the professions in the the EC

- National implementation of the provisions concerning recognition of higher national diplomas

  [*See Council Directive (EEC) 89/48*]

28.17 Standards

- Construction products

  [*See Com (87) 728 final OJ C30 4.2.88 p9*]

- electro-medical equipment
- gas appliances

  [*See Com (88) 786 final OJ C42 21.2.89 p5*]

- machinery safety
- measuring instruments
- medical devices

28.18 Telecommunications

- Common standards
- Application of competition provisions
- Development of Euro-wide services

[*See Com (88) 825 final*]

- Liberalisation of terminal equipment

[*See Council Directive (EEC) 88/301*]

- Harmonisation of the functions of PTTs
- Value-added services

[*See EC Commission Green Paper Com (87) 290*]

FACT FILE

USEFUL ADDRESSES

EC INSTITUTIONS

❑ **EC Commission**
Rue de la Loi, 200
1049-Brussels
Belgium
Tel : 16 322 235 1111

Information Offices
❑ *Dublin*
39 Moleworth Street
Dublin 2
Ireland
Tel : 01 712244

❑ *London*
Jean Monnet House
8 Storey's Gate
London SW1P 3AT
❑ *Belfast*
Windsor House
9/15 Bedford Street
Belfast BT2 7EG
❑ *Cardiff*
4 Cathedral Road
Cardiff CF1 9SG
❑ *Edinburgh*
7 Alva Street
Edinburgh EH2 4PH
Tel : 031 225 2058

❑ *Athens*
2 Vassilissis Sofias
PO Box 1102
Athina 1067A
Greece
❑ *Bonn*
Zitelmannstraße 22
5300 Bonn
Germany
❑ *Brussels*
Rue Archimède 73,
1040-Brussels
Belgium
❑ *Copenhagen*
Højbrohus
Østergade 61
Postbox 144
1004 København K
Denmark
❑ *The Hague*
Lange Voorhout 29
Den Haag

Netherlands
❑ *Lisbon*
35 rua do Sacramento à Lapa
1200 Lisboa
Portugal
❑ *Luxembourg*
Bâtiment Jean Monnet
Rue Alcide de Gasperi
2920 Luxembourg
❑ *Madrid*
Calle de Serrano 41
5a Planta
Madrid 1
Spain
❑ *Paris*
61, rue des Belles-Feuilles
75782 Paris Cedex 16
France
❑ *Rome*
Via Poli 29
00187 Roma
Italy

❑ **The Council of Ministers**
170, Rue de la Loi
B-1040 Brussels
Belgium

❑ **European Parliament**
Palais de l'Europe
Place Lenotre
Strasbourg
France
❑ Bâtiment Robert Schumann
Plateau du Kirchberg
Luxembourg
❑ 97-113 Rue Belliard
B-1040 Brussels
Belgium

Information Office
❑ *Dublin*
Jean Monnet Centre
43 Molesworth Street
Dublin 2
Tel : 01 719100

❒ **The European Court of Justice**
Luxembourg L-2920
Tel : 010 352 43031

OTHER CONTACTS

❒ **Council of Europe**
Avenue de L'Europe
B P 431 R6
F-67006
Strasbourg
France
Tel : 16 331 88 61 49 61

❒ **Chambers of Commerce of Ireland**
7 Clare Street
Dublin 2
Tel : 01 612888

❒ **Confederation of Irish Industry**
Confederation House
Kildare Street
Dublin 2
Tel : 01 779801
❒ **Brussels Office**
66 Ave. de Cortenberg
B-1040 Brussels
Belgium
Tel : 16 322 7631974

❒ **Customs and Excise**
Dublin Castle
Dublin 2
Tel : 01 792777

❒ **Department of Industry and Commerce**
Kildare Street
Dublin 2
Tel : 01 614444

❒ **Irish Business Bureau**
Ave de Cortenberg 66
1040 - Brussels
Belgium
Tel : 16 322 736 1974

❒ **Ministry of Agriculture and Food**
Agriculture House
Kildare Street
Dublin 2
Tel : 01 789011

❒ **Irish Intervention Agency**
Agriculture House
Kildare Street
Dublin 2
Tel : 01 789011

❒ **National Standards Association of Ireland**
c/o Eolas
Glasnevin
Dublin 9
Tel : 01 370101

118

PUBLICATIONS

OFFICIAL PUBLICATIONS

Official publications of the European Communities are obtainable from :

☐ **Office of Official Publications of the European Communities**
2 rue Mercier
L-2985 Luxembourg

Official outlets in the UK :
☐ *HMSO Publications Centre*
51 Nine Elms Lane
London SW8 5DR
Tel : 01 211 5656
☐ *Alan Armstrong & Associates*
2 Arkwright Road
Reading RG2 OSQ
Tel : 0734 751855

Legislation
☐ Official Journal of the European Communities "L" series (enacted legislation)
☐ Official Journal of the European Communities "C" series (proposed legislation)

Proceedings before the European Court of Justice
☐ European Court Reports
☐ Official Journal of the European Communities "C" series
☐ Transcripts of opinions and judgments and a weekly information sheet are available from :
European Court of Justice
Luxembourg L-2920

ON-LINE

CELEX / Context Legal Systems
LEXIS *(Butterworths)*

MAJOR WORKS, LAW REPORTS AND OTHER SERVICES

☐ Vaughan : Law of the European Communities
(1986 Butterworths)
☐ European Communities Legislation : Current Status
(1989 Butterworths)
☐ Encyclopaedia of European Community Law
(Sweet & Maxwell)
☐ Common Market Reporter
(CCH)
☐ Common Market Law Reports
(European Law Centre)
☐ Butterworths EC Brief

GENERAL TITLES

☐ CCH Guide to 1993
(1989 CCH)
☐ Collins : European Community Law in the United Kingdom
(1984 Butterworths)
☐ Deloittes : 1992
(1989 Butterworths)
☐ Lasok : European Court of Justice : Practice and Procedure
(1984 Butterworths)
☐ Lasok and Bridge : Law and Institutions of the European Communities
(1987 Butterworths)
☐ Lasok and Stone : Conflict of Laws in the European Communties
(1987 Butterworths)
☐ McMahon and Murphy : Application of European Community Law in Ireland
(1989 Butterworths)
☐ Steiner : Textbook on EEC Law
(1988 Blackstone Press Ltd)
☐ Wyatt & Dashwood : The Substantive Law of the EEC *(Sweet & Maxwell)*

The complete European package for the busy practitioner

Butterworths European Information Services

Butterworths European Information Services provides practitioners with the most up-to-date EC materials and information in whatever format is required on a regular basis

---
New Services

Butterworths EC Brief
- a weekly newsletter, with telephone enquiry service

Recent Publications

European Communities Legislation : Current Status
- an annual work, with quarterly supplements and telephone enquiry service, providing a complete guide to EC secondary legislation since 1952

Vaughan : Law of the European Communities
- major two volume work on the law and institutions of the European Communities

---

Research Services

General research services
- independent of any publications we will undertake any research into and provide any EC materials and information on request

Tailor-made services
- perhaps you require current full text materials and cases in a specific area, regular updates in only one or two Community law fields - bespoke research and monitoring services will be designed to satisfy your needs

Butterworths EC Law Locator

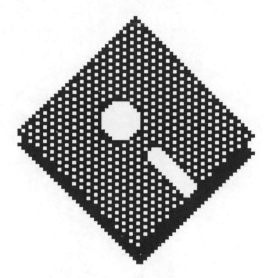

The simple, easy-to-use, quick search tool

You are dealing with a problem involving UK company law ,
immigration rules , social security provisons, employment law .....

You need to know the European provisions as well as the UK
provisions before you advise your clients

Just key in the subject area of your problem and the **Butterworths
EC Law Locator** will find all the relevant current references for
enacted and proposed EC legislation in that area

Disks formatted on request for IBM and IBM compatible systems

For further details about this and our other services please contact

Celia A. Trenton
Managing Editor, Butterworths European Information Services
88 Kingsway, London WC2B 6Ab
Tel : 031 405 6900   Fax : 031 405 1332

GLOSSARY AND ABBREVIATIONS

A

□ **ACP States**
African, Caribbean and Pacific states
- parties to the Lomé Convention
□ **accession**
admission to the Communities of a
state which was not a founding
member - process effected by an Act
of Accession
□ **adoption**
making of a measure having legal
effect
□ **advance fixing**
fixing of the amount of the levy or
refund on the import or export of
certain agricultural products prior to
a transaction is entered into
□ **aggregation and apportionment**
systems for calculating social
security benefits and dividing
responsibility for the payment of such
benefits between different member
states where appropriate
□ **annulment**
act declaring void an act of a
Community institution
□ **anti-dumping**
action against the dumping of goods
□ **approximation of laws**
adjustment of legislative or administrative provisions of member states
so that they accord with each other
□ **Assembly**
Community institution comprising
elected representatives from each
member state - commonly known as
the "European Parliament"
□ **association agreement**
agreement between the EC and one
or more third countries involving
reciprocal rights, obligations, actions
and procedures
□ **autonomous duty**
customs tariff fixed with a third
country or international organisation
other than by agreement

B

□ **basic price**
price used to determine the level of
market prices at which agricultural
products falling within certain

common organisation of markets
may be sold
□ **black clause**
clause causing an agreement to
infringe competition rules of lose
exempt status given by block exemption
□ **block exemption**
exemption from EEC Treaty, art 85(3)

C

□ **CAP**
common agricultural policy
□ **CCP**
common commercial policy
□ **CFI**
Court of First Instance
□ **CFP**
common fisheries policy
□ **CCT**
Common Customs Tariff
□ **CN**
Combined Nomenclature
□ **COREPER**
Committee of Permanent Representatives
□ **CTP**
common transport policy
□ **Chamber**
division in which the Court of Justice
sits when not sitting in plenary
session
□ **charges having equivalent effect**
pecuniary charge unilaterally
imposed on goods imported into one
member state from another
□ **comfort letter**
letter from an EC Commission
official stating that the Commission
intends to close the file on a case
involving possible infringement of
the EC competition rules
□ **Community agreement**
international agreement governing
matters which fall within
Community rather than member
state competence
□ **Community law**
law laid down in and derived from
the founding treaties
□ **Community transit**
regime governing movement of

goods through the Community
❏ **competition policy**
course of action adopted in order to maintain a desired level of rivalry between commercial undertakings
❏ **concentration**
collection together of market power
❏ **concerted practice**
co-ordination between undertakings which knowingly substitutes practical co-operation between them for the risks of competition
❏ **conjunctural policy**
policy intended to deal with cyclical problems of short-term economic trends
❏ **co-operation agreement**
- agreement between the EC and one or more third countries to co-operate in a certain field of activity
- agreement between two or more undertakings by which the parties agree to work together
❏ **co-ordination of laws**
see approximation of laws
❏ **countervailing measures**
charges or duties imposed on imports compensating for an advantage enjoyed by those goods in their country of origin
❏ **customs territory**
territory subject to a single customs regime

D
❏ **decision**
measure adopted by the EC Council or EC Commission which is binding in its entirety upon those to whom it is addressed
❏ **direct action**
contentious legal proceedings which commence and terminate in the European Court of Justice
❏ **direct applicability**
Community provision which becomes law in a member state without further national enactment
❏ **direct effect**
Community provision which confers upon individuals rights which national courts must protect
❏ **directive**
measure adopted by the EC Council or EC Commission which is binding upon each member state to which it is addressed as to the result to be achieved but which leaves the national authorities the choice of the form and methods to be used to achieve that result

❏ **drawback**
amount of customs duties repaid when the goods on which they are charged are exported
❏ **dumping**
introduction of a product from one country into another at less than the normal value of the product

E
❏ **EC**
European Communities
❏ **ECSC**
European Coal and Steel Community
❏ **ECJ**
European Court of Justice
❏ **ECU**
European Currency Unit
❏ **EEC**
European Economic Community
❏ **EMS**
European Monetary System
❏ **EP**
European Parliament
❏ **ESC**
Economic and Social Committee
❏ **EUA**
European Currency Unit
❏ **Euratom**
European Atomic Energy Community
❏ **external trade**
trade between the EC and third countries

F
❏ **founding members**
the members states who were signatory to the founding treaties, ie Belgium, France, Germany, Italy, Luxembourg and the Netherlands
❏ **founding treaties**
the three treaties which founded the Communities - ECSC Treaty, EEC Treaty and Euratom Treaty
❏ **four freedoms**
free movement of goods, persons, capital and the right of establishment and freedom to provide services

G
❏ **GATT**
General Agreement on Tariffs and Trade
❏ **generalised tariff preference**
grant of tariff advantages to a range of products from specified countries
❏ **green currency**
currency values used in the administration of the CAP

☐ guide price
price used in the common organisation of agricultural markets for intervention or imposition of import controls

H
☐ harmonisation of laws
see approximation of laws

I
☐ intervention agency
national body established to buy and sell agricultural products falling within the CAP
☐ intervention price
market price at which the producer of an agricultural product may sell it to an intervention agency instead of to another buyer in the market
☐ intra-Community trade
trade between member states
☐ inward processing
customs arrangement permitting goods to be admitted without payment of duties

J
☐ joint venture
undertaking jointly controlled by two or more independent undertakings

L
☐ legitimate expectation
legal entitlement to anticipate the occurrence of an event which is induced by the conduct of an administrative body
☐ Lomé
multilateral treaty giving preferential treatment to products originating from signatory states

M
☐ MCA
monetary compensatory amount
☐ measure having equivalent effect
national trading rule capable of hindering the free movement of goods between member states
☐ MINEX
fund designed to compensate ACP states for reductions in earnings from exports and minerals
☐ monetary compensatory amounts (MCAs)
subsidy or levy applied exports or imports of agricultural products in order to compensate for divergencies of currency exchange rates

N
☐ negative clearance
declaration by the EC Commission that on the basis of the facts before it there are no grounds under EC competition rules for action

O
☐ OECD
Organisation for Economic Co-operation and Development
☐ OJ
Official Journal of the European Communities
☐ OP
Office of Official Publications of the European Communities
☐ opinion
- act of EC Council or EC Commission which lacks binding force
- decision of ECJ under EEC Treaty, arts 95, 228
- reasoned statement made to the ECJ by an advocate general recommending to the court a solution of the issues of fact and law in a case pending before it
☐ order for reference
order made by national court or tribunal in the course of proceedings before it, suspending those proceedings before judgment and referring to the ECJ questions arising
☐ outward processing
customs arrangements under which goods are exported temporarily with a view to being reimported in the form of compensating products after they have undergone certain processing operations outside the customs territory
☐ overlapping of social security benefits
duplication of benefits payable under legislation of different member states
☐ own resources
financial resources of the Community derived from its own revenue

P
☐ preliminary ruling
decision of the ECJ on a point of EC law referred to it by a national Court or tribunal
☐ proportionality
the means used to attain a given end should not exceed what is appropriate to achieve that end

❒ **protective measure**
measures taken to protect the economy of a member state from economic difficulties

Q
❒ **quantitative restrictions**
measure imposing total or partial restraint on imports etc

R
❒ **recommendation**
- measure adopted by EC Council or EC Commission lacking binding force except when adopted under the ECSC Treaty
❒ **regulation**
measure adopted by EC Council or EC Commission which has general application, is binding in its entirety and has direct applicability in all members states

S
❒ **SAD**
Single Administrative Document
❒ **secondary legislation**
measures adopted by the Community institutions
❒ **STABEX**
Stabilisation of Export Earnings

T
❒ **target price**
price hoped producers of certain agricultural products will be able to obtain for their products
❒ **technical barriers to trade**
obstacles to trade derived from national consumer safety and environmental standards to which the goods must conform
❒ **third country**
state which is not a member of the EC
❒ **threshold price**
minimum import price for certain agricultural products

U
❒ **undertaking**
natural or legal person

TREATY OF ROME

TREATY ESTABLISHING THE EUROPEAN ECONOMIC COMMUNITY

Preamble (not reproduced here)

Part One - Principles

Part Two - Foundations of the Community
Title I - Free movement of goods
    Chapter 1 - The Customs Union
        Section 1-Elimination of customs duties between Member States
        Section 2-Setting up of the common customs tariff
    Chapter 2 - Elimination of quantitative restrictions between Member States

Title II - Agriculture

Title III - Free movement of persons, services and capital
    Chapter 1 - Workers
    Chapter 2 - Right of establishment
    Chapter 3 - Services
    Chapter 4 - Capital

Title IV - Transport

Part Three - Policy of the Community
Title I - Common rules
    Chapter 1 - Rules on competition
        Section 1 - Rules applying to undertakings
        Section 2 - Dumping
        Section 3 - Aids granted by States
    Chapter 2 - Tax provisions
    Chapter 3 - Approximation of laws

Title II - Economic policy
    Chapter 1 - Co-operation in economic and monetary policy
            (Economic andmonetary union)
    Chapter 2 - Conjunctural policy
    Chapter 3 - Balance of payments
    Chapter 4 - Commercial policy

Title III - Social policy
    Chapter 1 - Social provisions
    Chapter 2 - The European Social Fund

Title IV - The European Investment Bank

Title V - Economic and social cohesion

Title VI - Research and technological development

Title VII - Environment

Part Four - Association of the Overseas Countries and Territories

Part Five - Institutions of the Community
Title I - Provisions governing the institutions
    Chapter 1 - The institutions
        Section 1 - The European Parliament

Section 2 - The Council
Section 3 - The Commission
Section 4 - The Court of Justice
Chapter 2 - Provisions common to several institutions
Chapter 3 - The Economic and Social Committee.

Title II - Financial provisions

Part Six - General and final provisions
Setting up of the institutions
Final provisions

Annexes (not reproduced here)
Annex I -Lists A to G referred to in Articles 19 and 20 of this Treaty
Annex II-List referred to in Article 38 of this Treaty
Annex III-List of invisible transactions referred to in Article 106 of this Treaty
Annex IV-Overseas countries and territories to which the provisions of Part Four of this Treaty apply

PART ONE

PRINCIPLES

Article 1
By this Treaty, the High Contracting Parties establish among themselves a EUROPEAN ECONOMIC COMMUNITY.

Article 2
The Community shall have as its task, by establishing a common market and progressively approximating the economic policies of Member States, to promote throughout the Community a harmonious development of economic activities, a continuous and balanced expansion, an increase in stability, an accelerated raising of the standard of living and closer relations between the States belonging to it.

Article 3
For the purposes set out in Article 2, the activities of the Community shall include, as provided in this Treaty and in accordance with the timetable set out therein:

(a) the elimination, as between Member States, of customs duties and of quantitative restrictions on the import and export of goods, and of all other measures having equivalent effect;

(b) the establishment of a common customs tariff and of a common commercial policy towards third countries;

(c) the abolition, as between Member States, of obstacles to freedom of movement for persons, services and capital;

(d) the adoption of a common policy in the sphere of agriculture;

(e) the adoption of a common policy in the sphere of transport;

(f) the institution of a system ensuring that competition in the common market is not distorted;

(g) the application of procedures by which the economic policies of Member States can be co-ordinated and disequilibria in their balances of payments remedied;

(h) the approximation of the laws of Member States to the extent required for the proper functioning of the common market;

(i) the creation of a European Social Fund in order to improve employment opportunities for workers and to contribute to the raising of their standard of living;

(j) the establishment of a European Investment Bank to facilitate the economic expansion of the Community by opening up fresh resources;

(k) the association of the overseas countries and territories in order to increase trade and to promote jointly economic and social development.

Article 4
1. The tasks entrusted to the Community shall be carried out by the following institutions:

a European Parliament,
a Council,
a Commission,
a Court of Justice.

Each institution shall act within the limits of the powers conferred upon it by this Treaty.

2. The Council and the Commission shall be assisted by an Economic and Social Committee acting in an advisory capacity.

3. The audit shall be carried out by a Court of Auditors acting within the limits

of the powers conferred upon it by this Treaty.[1]

1 Paragraph 3 added by the Treaty amending Certain Financial Provisions, art 11

Article 5

Member States shall take all appropriate measures, whether general or particular, to ensure fulfilment of the obligations arising out of this Treaty or resulting from action taken by the institutions of the Community. They shall facilitate the achievement of the Community's tasks.

They shall abstain from any measure which could jeopardise the attainment of the objectives of this Treaty.

Article 6

1. Member States shall, in close co-operation with the institutions of the Community, co-ordinate their respective economic policies to the extent necessary to attain the objectives of this Treaty.

2. The institutions of the Community shall take care not to prejudice the internal and external financial stability of the Member States.

Article 7

Within the scope of application of this Treaty, and without prejudice to any special provisions contained therein, any discrimination on grounds of nationality shall be prohibited.

The Council may, on a proposal from the Commission and in co-operation with the European Parliament, adopt, by a qualified majority, rules designed to prohibit such discrimination.[1]

1 As amended by the Single European Act, art 6 (2).

Article 8

1. The common market shall be progressively established during a transitional period of twelve years.

This transitional period shall be divided into three stages of four years each; the length of each stage may be altered in accordance with the provisions set out below.

2. To each stage there shall be assigned a set of actions to be initiated and carried through concurrently.

3. Transition from the first to the second stage shall be conditional upon a finding that the objectives specifically laid down in this Treaty for the first stage have in fact been attained in substance and that, subject to the exceptions and procedures provided for in this Treaty, the obligations have been fulfilled.

This finding shall be made at the end of the fourth year by the Council, acting unanimously on a report from the Commission. A Member State may not, however, prevent unanimity by relying upon the non-fulfilment of its own obligations. Failing unanimity, the first stage shall automatically be extended for one year.

At the end of the fifth year, the Council shall make its finding under the same conditions. Failing unanimity, the first stage shall automatically be extended for a further year.

At the end of the sixth year, the Council shall make its finding, acting by a qualified majority on a report from the Commission.

4. Within one month of the last-mentioned vote any Member State which voted with the minority or, if the required majority was not obtained, any Member State shall be entitled to call upon the Council to appoint an arbitration board whose decision shall binding upon all Member States and upon the institutions of the Community. The arbitration board shall consist of three members appointed by the Council acting unanimously on a proposal from the Commission.

If the Council has not appointed the members of the arbitration board within one month of being called upon to do so, they shall be appointed by the Court of Justice within a further period of one month.

The arbitration board shall elect its own Chairman.

The board shall make its award within six months of the date of the Council vote referred to in the last sub-paragraph of paragraph 3.

5. The second and third stages may not be extended or curtailed except by a decision of the Council, acting unanimously on a proposal from the Commission.

6. Nothing in the preceding paragraphs shall cause the transitional period to last more than fifteen years after the entry into force of this Treaty.

7. Save for the exceptions or derogations provided for in this Treaty, the expiry of the transitional period shall constitute the latest date by which all the rules laid down must enter into force and all the measures required for establishing the common market must be implemented.

Article 8a [1]
The Community shall adopt measures with the aim of progressively establishing the internal market over a period expiring on 31 December 1992, in accordance with the provisions of this Article and of Articles 8b, 8c, 28, 57 (2), 59, 70 (1), 84, 99, 100a and 100b and without prejudice to the other provisions of this Treaty.

The internal market shall comprise an area without internal frontiers in which the free movement of goods, persons, services and capital is ensured in accordance with the provisions of this Treaty.

1 Added by the Single European Act, art 13.

Article 8b [1]
The Commission shall report to the Council before 31 December 1988 and again before 31 December 1990 on the progress made towards achieving the internal market within the time limit fixed in Article 8a.

The Council, acting by a qualified majority on a proposal from the Commission, shall determine the guidelines and conditions necessary to ensure balanced progress in all the sectors concerned.

1 Added by the Single European Act, art 14.

Article 8c [1]
When drawing up its proposals with a view to achieving the objectives set out in article 8a, the Commission shall take into account the extent of the effort that certain economies showing differences in development will have to sustain during the period of establishment of the internal market and it may propose appropriate provisions.

If these provisions take the form of derogations, they must be of a temporary

132

nature and must cause the least possible disturbance to the functioning of the common market.

---

1 Added by the Single European Act, art 15.

PART TWO

FOUNDATIONS OF THE COMMUNITY

TITLE I
FREE MOVEMENT OF GOODS

Article 9

1. The Community shall be based upon a customs union which shall cover all trade in goods and which shall involve the prohibition between Member States of customs duties on imports and exports and of all charges having equivalent effect, and the adoption of a common customs tariff in their relations with third countries.

2. The provisions of Chapter 1, Section 1, and of Chapter 2 of this Title shall apply to products originating in Member States and to products coming from third countries which are in free circulation in Member States.

Article 10

1. Products coming from a third country shall be considered to be in free circulation in a Member State if the import formalities have been complied with and any customs duties or charges having equivalent effect which are payable have been levied in that Member State, and if they have not benefited from a total or partial drawback of such duties or charges.

2. The Commission shall, before the end of the first year after the entry into force of this Treaty, determine the methods of administrative co-operation to be adopted for the purpose of applying Article 9 (2), taking into account the need to reduce as much as possible formalities imposed on trade.

Before the end of the first year after the entry into force of this Treaty, the Commission shall lay down the provisions applicable, as regards trade between Member States, to goods originating in another Member State in whose manufacture products have been used on which the exporting Member State has not levied the appropriate customs duties or charges having equivalent effect, or which have benefitted from a total or partial drawback of such duties or charges.

In adopting these provisions, the Commission shall take into account the rules for the elimination of customs duties within the Community and for the progressive application of the common customs tariff.

Article 11

Member States shall take all appropriate measures to enable Governments to carry out, within the periods of time laid down, the obligations with regard to customs duties which devolve upon them pursuant to this Treaty.

CHAPTER 1-THE CUSTOMS UNION
Section 1-Elimination of customs duties between Member States

Article 12

Member States shall refrain from introducing between themselves any new customs duties on imports or exports or any charges having equivalent effect, and from increasing those which they already apply in their trade with each other.

Article 13

1. Customs duties on imports in force between Member States shall be progressively abolished by them during the transitional period in accordance with Articles 14 and 15.

2. Charges having an effect equivalent to customs duties on imports, in force between Member States, shall be progressively abolished by them during the transitional period. The Commission shall determine by means of directives the timetable for such abolition. It shall be guided by the rules contained in Article 14 (2) and (3) and by the directives issued by the Council pursuant to Article 14 (2).

Article 14

1. For each product, the basic duty to which the successive reductions shall be applied shall be the duty applied on 1 January 1957.

2. The timetable for the reductions shall be determined as follows:

(a)   during the first stage, the first reduction shall be made one year after the date when this Treaty enters into force; the second reduction, eighteen months later; the third reduction, at the end of the fourth year after the date when this Treaty enters into force;

(b)   during the second stage, a reduction shall be made eighteen months after that stage begins; a second reduction, eighteen months after the preceding one; a third reduction, one year later;

(c)   any remaining reductions shall be made during the third stage; the Council shall, acting by a qualified majority on a proposal from the Commission, determine the timetable therefor by means of directives.

3. At the time of the first reduction, Member States shall introduce between themselves a duty on each product equal to the basic duty minus 10%.

At the time of each subsequent reduction, each Member State shall reduce its customs duties as a whole in such manner as to lower by 10% its total customs receipts as defined in paragraph 4 and to reduce the duty on each product by at least 5% of the basic duty.

In the case, however, of products on which the duty is still in excess of 30%, each reduction must be at least 10 per cent of the basic duty.

4. The total customs receipts of each Member State, as referred to in paragraph 3, shall be calculated by multiplying the value of its imports from other Member States during 1956 by the basic duties.

5. Any special problems raised in applying paragraphs 1 to 4 shall be settled by directives issued by the Council acting by a qualified majority on a proposal from the Commission.

6. Member States shall report to the Commission on the manner in which effect has been given to the preceding rules for the reduction of duties. They shall endeavour to ensure that the reduction made in the duties on each product shall amount:
- at the end of the first stage, to at least 25% of the basic duty;
- at the end of the second stage, to at least 50% of the basic duty.

If the Commission finds that there is a risk that the objectives laid down in Article 13, and the percentages laid down in this paragraph, cannot be attained, it shall make all appropriate recommendations to Member States.

7. The provisions of this Article may be amended by the Council, acting unanimously on a proposal from the Commission and after consulting the EuropeanParliament.

Article 15

1. Irrespective of the provisions of Article 14, any Member State may, in the course of the transitional period, suspend in whole or in part the collection of duties applied by it to products imported from other Member States. It shall inform the other Member States and the Commission thereof.

2. The Member States declare their readiness to reduce customs duties against the other Member States more rapidly than is provided for in Article 14 if their general economic situation and the situation of the economic sector concerned so permit.

To this end, the Commission shall make recommendations to the Member States concerned.

Article 16

Member States shall abolish between themselves customs duties on exports and charges having equivalent effect by the end of the first stage at the latest.

Article 17

1. The provisions of Articles 9 to 15 (1) shall also apply to customs duties of a fiscal nature. Such duties shall not, however, be taken into consideration for the purpose of calculating either total customs receipts or the reduction of customs duties as a whole as referred to in Article 14 (3) and (4).

Such duties shall, at each reduction, be lowered by not less than 10% of the basic duty. Member States may reduce such duties more rapidly than is provided for in Article 14.

2. Member States shall, before the end of the first year after the entry into force of this Treaty, inform the Commission of their customs duties of a fiscal nature.

3. Member States shall retain the right to substitute for these duties an internal tax which complies with the provisions of Article 95.

4. If the Commission finds that substitution for any customs duty of a fiscal nature meets with serious difficulties in a Member State, it shall authorise that State to retain the duty on condition that it shall abolish it not later than six years after the entry into force of this Treaty. Such authorisation must be applied for before the end of the first year after the entry into force of this Treaty.

Section 2-Setting up of the common customs tariff

Article 18

The Member States declare their readiness to contribute to the development of international trade and the lowering of barriers to trade by entering into agreements designed, on a basis of reciprocity and mutual advantage, to reduce customs duties below the general level of which they could avail themselves as a result of the establishment of a customs union between them.

Article 19

1. Subject to the conditions and within the limits provided for hereinafter,

duties in the common customs tariff shall be at the level of the arithmetical average of the duties applied in the four customs territories comprised in the Community.

2. The duties taken as the basis for calculating this average shall be those applied by Member States on 1 January 1957.

In the case of the Italian tariff, however, the duty applied shall be that without the temporary 10% reduction. Furthermore, with respect to items on which the Italian tariff contains a conventional duty, this duty shall be substituted for the duty applied as defined above, provided that it does not exceed the latter by more than 10%. Where the conventional duty exceeds the duty applied as defined above by more than 10%, the latter duty plus 10% shall be taken as the basis for calculating the arithmetical average.

With regard to the tariff headings in List A, the duties shown in that List shall, for the purpose of calculating the arithmetical average, be substituted for the duties applied.

3. The duties in the common customs tariff shall not exceed:
    (a)   3% for products within the tariff headings in List B;
    (b)   10% for products within the tariff headings in List C;
    (c)   15% for products within the tariff headings in List D;
    (d)   25% for products within the tariff headings in List E; where, in respect of such products, the tariff of the Benelux countries contains a duty not exceeding 3%, such duty shall, for the purpose of calculating the arithmetical average, be raised to 12%.

4. List F prescribes the duties applicable to the products listed therein.

5. The Lists of tariff headings referred to in this Article and in Article 20 are set out in Annex I to this Treaty.

Article 20

The duties applicable to the products in List G shall be determined by negotiation between the Member States. Each Member State may add further products to this List to a value not exceeding 2% of the total value of its imports from third countries in the course of the year 1956.

The Commission shall take all appropriate steps to ensure that such negotiations shall be undertaken before the end of the second year after the entry into force of this Treaty and be concluded before the end of the first stage.

If, for certain products, no agreement can be reached within these periods, the Council shall, on a proposal from the Commission, acting unanimously until the end of the second stage and by a qualified majority thereafter, determine the duties in the common customs tariff.

Article 21

1. Technical difficulties which may arise in applying Articles 19 and 20 shall be resolved, within two years of the entry into force of this Treaty, by directives issued by the Council acting by a qualified majority on a proposal from the Commission.

2. Before the end of the first stage, or at latest when the duties are determined, the Council shall, acting by a qualified majority on a proposal from the Commission, decide on any adjustments required in the interests of the internal consistency of the common customs tariff as a result of applying the rules set out in Articles 19 and 20, taking account in particular of the degree

of processing undergone by the various goods to which the common tariff applies.

Article 22
The Commission shall, within two years of the entry into force of this Treaty, determine the extent to which the customs duties of a fiscal nature referred to in Article 17 (2) shall be taken into account in calculating the arithmetical average provided for in Article 19 (1). The Commission shall take account of any protective character which such duties may have.

Within six months of such determination, any Member State may request that the procedure provided for in Article 20 should be applied to the product in question, but in this event the percentage limit provided in that Article shall not be applicable to that State.

Article 23
1. For the purpose of the progressive introduction of the common customs tariff, Member States shall amend their tariffs applicable to third countries as follows:

(a) in the case of tariff headings on which the duties applied in practice on 1 January 1957 do not differ by more than 15% in either direction from the duties in the common customs tariff, the latter duties shall be applied at the end of the fourth year after the entry into force of this Treaty;

(b) in any other case, each Member State shall, as from the same date, apply a duty reducing by 30% the difference between the duty applied in practice on 1 January 1957 and the duty in the common customs tariff;

(c) at the end of the second stage this difference shall again be reduced by 30%;

(d) in the case of tariff headings for which the duties in the common customs tariff are not yet available at the end of the first stage, each Member State shall, within six months of the Council's action in accordance with Article 20, apply such duties as would result from application of the rules contained in this paragraph.

2. Where a Member State has been granted an authorisation under Article 17(4), it need not, for as long as that authorisation remains valid, apply the preceding provisions to the tariff headings to which the authorisation applies. When such authorisation expires, the Member State concerned shall apply such duty as would have resulted from application of the rules contained in paragraph 1.

3. The common customs tariff shall be applied in its entirety by the end of the transitional period at the latest.

Article 24
Member States shall remain free to change their duties more rapidly than is provided for in Article 23 in order to bring them into line with the common customs tariff.

Article 25
1. If the Commission finds that the production in Member States of particular products contained in Lists B, C and D is insufficient to supply the demands of one of the Member States, and that such supply traditionally depends to a considerable extent on imports from third countries, the Council shall, acting by a qualified majority on a proposal from the Commission, grant the Member State concerned tariff quotas at a reduced rate of duty or duty free.

Such quotas may not exceed the limits beyond which the risk might arise of activities being transferred to the detriment of other Member States.

2. In the case of the products in List E, and of those in List G for which the rates of duty have been determined in accordance with the procedure provided for in the third paragraph of Article 20, the Commission shall, where a change in sources of supply or shortage of supplies within the Community is such as to entail harmful consequences for the processing industries of a Member State, at the request of that Member State, grant it tariff quotas at a reduced rate of duty or duty free.

Such quotas may not exceed the limits beyond which the risk might arise of activities being transferred to the detriment of other Member States.

3. In the case of the products listed in Annex II to this Treaty, the Commission may authorise any Member State to suspend, in whole or in part, collection of the duties applicable or may grant such Member State tariff quotas at a reduced rate of duty or duty free, provided that no serious disturbance of the market of the products concerned results therefrom.

4. The Commission shall periodically examine tariff quotas granted pursuant to this Article.

Article 26
The Commission may authorise any Member State encountering special difficulties to postpone the lowering or raising of duties provided for in Article 23 in respect of particular headings in its tariff.

Such authorisation may only be granted for a limited period and in respect of tariff headings which, taken together, represent for such State not more than 5% of the value of its imports from third countries in the course of the latest year for which statistical data are available.

Article 27
Before the end of the first stage, Member States shall, in so far as may be necessary, take steps to approximate their provisions laid down by law, regulation or administrative action in respect of customs matters. To this end, the Commission shall make all appropriate recommendations to Member States.

Article 28
Any autonomous alteration or suspension of duties in the common customs tariff shall be decided by the Council acting by a qualified majority on a proposal from the Commission.[1]

1 As substituted by the Single European Act, art 16(1).

Article 29
In carrying out the tasks entrusted to it under this Section the Commission shall be guided by:
- (a) the need to promote trade between Member States and third countries;
- (b) developments in conditions of competition within the Community in so far as they lead to an improvement in the competitive capacity of undertakings;
- (c) the requirements of the Community as regards the supply of raw materials and semi-finished goods; in this connection the Commission shall take care to avoid distorting conditions of competition between Member States in respect of finished goods;
- (d) the need to avoid serious disturbances in the economies of Member States and to ensure rational development of

production and an expansion of consumption within the Community.

CHAPTER 2-ELIMINATION OF QUANTITATIVE RESTRICTIONS BETWEEN MEMBER STATES

Article 30
Quantitative restrictions on imports and all measures having equivalent effect shall, without prejudice to the following provisions, be prohibited between Member States.

Article 31
Member States shall refrain from introducing between themselves any new quantitative restrictions or measures having equivalent effect.

This obligation shall, however, relate only to the degree of liberalisation attained in pursuance of the decisions of the Council of the organisation for European Economic Co-operation of 14 January 1955. Member States shall supply the Commission, not later than six months after the entry into force of this Treaty, with lists of the products liberalised by them in pursuance of these decisions. These lists shall be consolidated between Member States.

Article 32
In their trade with one another Member States shall refrain from making more restrictive the quotas and measures having equivalent effect existing at the date of the entry into force of this Treaty.

These quotas shall be abolished by the end of the transitional period at the latest. During that period, they shall be progressively abolished in accordance with the following provisions.

Article 33
1. One year after the entry into force of this Treaty, each Member State shall convert any bilateral quotas open to any other Member States into global quotas open without discrimination to all other Member States.

On the same date, Member States shall increase the aggregate of the global quotas so established in such a manner as to bring about an increase of not less than 20% in their total value as compared with the preceding year. The global quota for each product, however, shall be increased by not less than 10%.

The quotas shall be increased annually in accordance with the same rules and in the same proportions in relation to the preceding year.

The fourth increase shall take place at the end of the fourth year after the entry into force of this Treaty; the fifth, one year after the beginning of the second stage.

2. Where, in the case of a product which has not been liberalised, the global quota does not amount to 3% of the national production of the State concerned, a quota equal to not less than 3% of such national production shall be introduced not later than one year after the entry into force of this Treaty. This quota shall be raised to 4% at the end of the second year, and to 5% at the end of the third. Thereafter, the Member State concerned shall increase the quota by not less than 15% annually.

Where there is no such national production, the Commission shall take a decision establishing an appropriate quota.

139

3. At the end of the tenth year, each quota shall be equal to not less than 20% of the national production.

4. If the Commission finds by means of a decision that during two successive years the imports of any product have been below the level of the quota opened, this global quota shall not be taken into account in calculating the total value of the global quotas. In such case, the Member State shall abolish quota restrictions on the product concerned.

5. In the case of quotas representing more than 20% of the national production of the product concerned, the Council may, acting by a qualified majority on a proposal from the Commission, reduce the minimum percentage of 10% laid down in paragraph 1. This alteration shall not, however, affect the obligation to increase the total value of global quotas by 20% annually.

6. Member States which have exceeded their obligations as regards the degree of liberalisation attained in pursuance of the decisions of the Council of the organisation for European Economic Co-operation of 14 January 1955 shall be entitled, when calculating the annual total increase of 20% provided for in paragraph 1, to take into account the amount of imports liberalised by autonomous action. Such calculation shall be submitted to the Commission for its prior approval.

7. The Commission shall issue directives establishing the procedure and timetable in accordance with which Member States shall abolish, as between themselves, any measures in existence when this Treaty enters into force which have an effect equivalent to quotas.

8. If the Commission finds that the application of the provisions of this Article, and in particular of the provisions concerning percentages, makes it impossible to ensure that the abolition of quotas provided for in the second paragraph of Article 32 is carried out progressively, the Council may, on a proposal from the Commission, acting unanimously during the first stage and by a qualified majority thereafter, amend the procedure laid down in this Article and may, in particular, increase the percentages fixed.

Article 34
1. Quantitative restrictions on exports, and all measures having equivalent effect, shall be prohibited between Member States.

2. Member States shall, by the end of the first stage at the latest, abolish all quantitative restrictions on exports and any measures having equivalent effect which are in existence when this Treaty enters into force.

Article 35
The Member States declare their readiness to abolish quantitative restrictions on imports from and exports to other Member States more rapidly than is provided for in the preceding Articles, if their general economic situation and the situation of the economic sector concerned so permit.

To this end, the Commission shall make recommendations to the Member States concerned.

Article 36
The provisions of Articles 30 to 34 shall not preclude prohibitions or restrictions on imports, exports or goods in transit justified on grounds of public morality, public policy or public security; the protection of health and life of humans, animals or plants; the protection of national treasures possessing artistic, historic or archaeological value; or the protection of industrial and commercial property. Such prohibitions or restrictions shall not, however, constitute a means of arbitrary discrimination or a disguised restriction on trade between Member States.

Article 37

1. Member States shall progressively adjust any State monopolies of a commercial character so as to ensure that when the transitional period has ended no discrimination regarding the conditions under which goods are procured and marketed exists between nationals of Member States.

The provisions of this Article shall apply to any body through which a Member State, in law or in fact, either directly or indirectly supervises, determines or appreciably influences imports or exports between Member States. These provisions shall likewise apply to monopolies delegated by the State to others.

2. Member States shall refrain from introducing any new measure which is contrary to the principles laid down in paragraph 1 or which restricts the scope of the Articles dealing with the abolition of customs duties and quantitative restrictions between Member States.

3. The timetable for the measures referred to in paragraph 1 shall be harmonised with the abolition of quantitative restrictions on the same products provided for in Articles 30 to 34.

If a product is subject to a State monopoly of a commercial character in only one or some Member States, the Commission may authorise the other Member States to apply protective measures until the adjustment provided for in paragraph 1 has been effected; the Commission shall determine the conditions and details of such measures.

4. If a State monopoly of a commercial character has rules which are designed to make it easier to dispose of agricultural products or obtain for them the best return, steps should be taken in applying the rules contained in this Article to ensure equivalent safeguards for the employment and standard of living of the producers concerned, account being taken of the adjustments that will be possible and the specialisation that will be needed with the passage of time.

5. The obligations on Member States shall be binding only in so far as they are compatible with existing international agreements.

6. With effect from the first stage the Commission shall make recommendations as to the manner in which and the timetable according to which the adjustment provided for in this Article shall be carried out.

TITLE II
AGRICULTURE

Article 38

1. The common market shall extend to agriculture and trade in agricultural products. "Agricultural products" means the products of the soil, of stockfarming and of fisheries and products of first-stage processing directly related to these products.

2. Save as otherwise provided in Articles 39 to 46, the rules laid down for the establishment of the common market shall apply to agricultural products.

3. The products subject to the provisions of Articles 39 to 46 are listed in Annex II to this Treaty. Within two years of the entry into force of this Treaty, however, the Council shall, acting by a qualified majority on a proposal from the Commission, decide what products are to be added to this list.

4. The operation and development of the common market for agricultural

141

products must be accompanied by the establishment of a common agricultural policy among the Member States.

Article 39
1. The objectives of the common agricultural policy shall be:
    (a)   to increase agricultural productivity by promoting technical progress and by ensuring the rational development of agricultural production and the optimum utilisation of the factors of production, in particular labour;
    (b)   thus to ensure a fair standard of living for the agricultural community, in particular by increasing the individual earnings of persons engaged in agriculture;
    (c)   to stabilise markets;
    (d)   to assure the availability of supplies;
    (e)   to ensure that supplies reach consumers at reasonable prices.

2. In working out the common agricultural policy and the special methods for its application, account shall be taken of:
    (a)   the particular nature of agricultural activity, which results from the social structure of agriculture and from structural and natural disparities between the various agricultural regions;
    (b)   the need to effect the appropriate adjustments by degrees;
    (c)   the fact that in the Member States agriculture constitutes a sector closely linked with the economy as a whole.

Article 40
1. Member States shall develop the common agricultural policy by degrees during the transitional period and shall bring it into force by the end of that period at the latest.

2. In order to attain the objectives set out in Article 39 a common organisation of agricultural markets shall be established.

This organisation shall take one of the following forms, depending on the product concerned:
    (a)   common rules on competition;
    (b)   compulsory co-ordination of the various national market organisations;
    (c)   a European market organisation.

3. The common organisation established in accordance with paragraph 2 may include all measures required to attain the objectives set out in Article 39, in particular regulation of prices, aids for the production and marketing of the various products, storage and carry-over arrangements and common machinery for stabilising imports or exports.

The common organisation shall be limited to pursuit of the objectives set out in Article 39 and shall exclude any discrimination between producers or consumers within the Community.

Any common price policy shall be based on common criteria and uniform methods of calculation.

4. In order to enable the common organisation referred to in paragraph 2 to attain its objectives, one or more agricultural guidance and guarantee funds may be set up.

Article 41
To enable the objectives set out in Article 39 to be attained, provision may

be made within the framework of the common agricultural policy for measures such as:

(a)   an effective co-ordination of efforts in the spheres of vocational training, of research and of the dissemination of agricultural knowledge; this may include joint financing of projects or institutions;

(b)   joint measures to promote consumption of certain products.

Article 42

The provisions of the Chapter relating to rules on competition shall apply to production of and trade in agricultural products only to the extent determined by the Council within the framework of Article 43 (2) and (3) and in accordance with the procedure laid down therein, account being taken of the objectives set out in Article 39.

The Council may, in particular, authorise the granting of aid:

(a)   for the protection of enterprises handicapped by structural or natural conditions;

(b)   within the framework of economic development programmes.

Article 43

1. In order to evolve the broad lines of a common agricultural policy, the Commission shall, immediately this Treaty enters into force, convene a conference of the Member States with a view to making a comparison of their agricultural policies, in particular by producing a statement of their resources and needs.

2. Having taken into account the work of the conference provided for in paragraph 1, after consulting the Economic and Social Committee and within two years of the entry into force of this Treaty, the Commission shall submit proposals for working out and implementing the common agricultural policy, including the replacement of the national organisations by one of the forms of common organisation provided for in Article 40 (2), and for implementing the measures specified in this Title.

These proposals shall take account of the interdependence of the agricultural matters mentioned in this Title.

The Council shall, on a proposal from the Commission and after consulting the European Parliament, acting unanimously during the first two stages and by a qualified majority thereafter, make regulations, issue directives, or take decisions, without prejudice to any recommendations it may also make.

3. The Council may, acting by a qualified majority and in accordance with paragraph 2, replace the national market organisations by the common organisation provided for in Article 40 (2) if:

(a)   the common organisation offers Member States which are opposed to this measure and which have an organisation of their own for the production in question equivalent safeguards for the employment and standard of living of the producers concerned, account being taken of the adjustments that will be possible and the specialisation that will be needed with the passage of time;

(b)   such an organisation ensures conditions for trade within the Community similar to those existing in a national market.

4. If a common organisation for certain raw materials is established before a common organisation exists for the corresponding processed products, such raw materials as are used for processed products intended for export to third countries may be imported from outside the Community.

Article 44

1. In so far as progressive abolition of customs duties and quantitative restrictions between Member States may result in prices likely to jeopardise the attainment of the objectives set out in Article 39, each Member State shall, during the transitional period, be entitled to apply to particular products, in a non-discriminatory manner and in substitution for quotas and to such an extent as shall not impede the expansion of the volume of trade provided for in Article 45 (2), a system of minimum prices below which imports may be either:

    - temporarily suspended or reduced; or
    - allowed, but subjected to the condition that they are made at a price higher than the minimum price for the product concerned.

In the latter case the minimum prices shall not include customs duties.

2. Minimum prices shall neither cause a reduction of the trade existing between Member States when this Treaty enters into force nor form an obstacle to progressive expansion of this trade. Minimum prices shall not be applied so as to form an obstacle to the development of a natural preference between Member States.

3. As soon as this Treaty enters into force the Council shall, on a proposal from the Commission, determine objective criteria for the establishment of minimum price systems and for the fixing of such prices.

These criteria shall in particular take account of the average national production costs in the Member State applying the minimum price, of the position of the various undertakings concerned in relation to such average production costs, and of the need to promote both the progressive improvement of agricultural practice and the adjustments and specialisation needed within the common market.

The Commission shall further propose a procedure for revising these criteria in order to allow for and speed up technical progress and to approximate prices progressively within the common market.

These criteria and the procedure for revising them shall be determined by the Council acting unanimously within three years of the entry into force of this Treaty.

4. Until the decision of the Council takes effect, Member States may fix minimum prices on condition that these are communicated beforehand to the Commission and to the other Member States so that they may submit their comments.

Once the Council has taken its decision, Member States shall fix minimum prices on the basis of the criteria determined as above.

The Council may, acting by a qualified majority on a proposal from the Commission, rectify any decisions taken by Member States which do not conform to the criteria defined above.

5. If it does not prove possible to determine the said objective criteria for certain products by the beginning of the third stage, the Council may, acting by a qualified majority on a proposal from the Commission, vary the minimum prices applied to these products.

6. At the end of the transitional period, a table of minimum prices still in force shall be drawn up. The Council shall, acting on a proposal from the Commission and by a majority of nine votes in accordance with the weighting laid down in the first subparagraph of Article 148 (2), determine the system

to be applied within the framework of the common agricultural policy.

Article 45
1. Until national market organisations have been replaced by one of the forms of common organisation referred to in Article 40 (2), trade in products in respect of which certain Member States:
  - have arrangements designed to guarantee national producers a market for their products; and
  - are in need of imports,
shall be developed by the conclusion of long-term agreements or contracts between importing and exporting Member States.

These agreements or contracts shall be directed towards the progressive abolition of any discrimination in the application of these arrangements to the various producers within the Community.

Such agreements or contracts shall be concluded during the first stage; account shall be taken of the principle of reciprocity.

2. As regards quantities, these agreements or contracts shall be based on the average volume of trade between Member States in the products concerned during the three years before the entry into force of this Treaty and shall provide for an increase in the volume of trade within the limits of existing requirements, account being taken of traditional patterns of trade.

As regards prices, these agreements or contracts shall enable producers to dispose of the agreed quantities at prices which shall be progressively approximated to those paid to national producers on the domestic market of the purchasing country.

This approximation shall proceed as steadily as possible and shall be completed by the end of the transitional period at the latest.

Prices shall be negotiated between the parties concerned within the framework of directives issued by the Commission for the purpose of implementing the two preceding sub-paragraphs.

If the first stage is extended, these agreements or contracts shall continue to be carried out in accordance with the conditions applicable at the end of the fourth year after the entry into force of this Treaty, the obligation to increase quantities and to approximate prices being suspended until the transition to the second stage.

Member States shall avail themselves of any opportunity open to them under their legislation, particularly in respect of import policy, to ensure the conclusion and carrying out of these agreements or contracts.

3. To the extent that Member States require raw materials for the manufacture of products to be exported outside the Community in competition with products of third countries, the above agreements or contracts shall not form an obstacle to the importation of raw materials for this purpose from third countries. This provision shall not, however, apply if the Council unanimously decides to make provision for payments required to compensate for the higher price paid on goods imported for this purpose on the basis of these agreements or contracts in relation to the delivered price of the same goods purchased on the world market.

Article 46
Where in a Member State a product is subject to a national market organisation or to internal rules having equivalent effect which affect the competitive position of similar production in another Member State, a countervailing

charge shall be applied by Member States to imports of this product coming from the Member State where such organisation or rules exist, unless that State applies a countervailing charge on export.

The Commission shall fix the amount of these charges at the level required to redress the balance; it may also authorise other measures, the conditions and details of which it shall determine.

Article 47
As to the functions to be performed by the Economic and Social Committee in pursuance of this Title, its agricultural section shall hold itself at the disposal of the Commission to prepare, in accordance with the provisions of Articles 197 and 198, the deliberations of the Committee.

TITLE III
FREE MOVEMENT OF PERSONS, SERVICES AND CAPITAL

CHAPTER 1-WORKERS

Article 48
1. Freedom of movement for workers shall be secured within the Community by the end of the transitional period at the latest.

2. Such freedom of movement shall entail the abolition of any discrimination based on nationality between workers of the Member States as regards employment, remuneration and other conditions of work and employment.

3. It shall entail the right, subject to limitations justified on grounds of public policy, public security or public health:

    (a)   to accept offers of employment actually made;
    (b)   to move freely within the territory of Member States for this purpose;
    (c)   to stay in a Member State for the purpose of employment in accordance with the provisions governing the employment of nationals of that State laid down by law, regulation or administrative action;
    (d)   to remain in the territory of a Member State after having been employed in that State, subject to conditions which shall be embodied in implementing regulations to be drawn up by the Commission.

4. The provisions of this Article shall not apply to employment in the public service.

Article 49
As soon as this Treaty enters into force, the Council shall, acting by a qualified majority on a proposal from the Commission, in co-operation with the European Parliament and after consulting the Economic and Social Committee, issue directives or make regulations setting out the measures required to bring about, by progressive stages, freedom of movement for workers, as defined in Article 48, in particular:[1]

    (a)   by ensuring close co-operation between national employment services;
    (b)   by systematically and progressively abolishing those administrative procedures and practices and those qualifying periods in respect of eligibility for available employment, whether resulting from national legislation or from agreements previously concluded between Member States, the maintenance of which would form an obstacle to

liberalisation of the movement of workers;
(c)   by systematically and progressively abolishing all such
        qualifying periods and other restrictions provided for either
        under national legislation or under agreements previously
        concluded between Member States as imposed on workers of
        other Member States conditions regarding the free choice of
        employment other than those imposed on workers of the
        State concerned;
(d)   by setting up appropriate machinery to bring offers of
        employment into touch with applications for employment
        and to facilitate the achievement of a balance between supply
        and demand in the employment market in such a way as to
        avoid serious threats to the standard of living and level of
        employment in the various regions and industries.

1 As amended by the Single European Act, art 6(3).

Article 50
Member States shall, within the framework of a joint programme, encourage the exchange of young workers.

Article 51
The Council shall, acting unanimously on a proposal from the Commission, adopt such measures in the field of social security as are necessary to provide freedom of movement for workers; to this end, it shall make arrangements to secure for migrant workers and their dependants:
(a)   aggregation, for the purpose of acquiring and retaining the
        right to benefit and of calculating the amount of benefit, of all
        periods taken into account under the laws of the several
        countries;
(b)   payment of benefits to persons resident in the territories of
        Member States.

CHAPTER 2-RIGHT OF ESTABLISHMENT

Article 52
Within the framework of the provisions set out below, restrictions on the freedom of establishment of nationals of a Member State in the territory of another Member State shall be abolished by progressive stages in the course of the transitional period. Such progressive abolition shall also apply to restrictions on the setting up of agencies, branches or subsidiaries by nationals of any Member State established in the territory of any Member State.

Freedom of establishment shall include the right to take up and pursue activities as self-employed persons and to set up and manage undertakings, in particular companies or firms within the meaning of the second paragraph of Article 58, under the conditions laid down for its own nationals by the law of the country where such establishment is effected, subject to the provisions of the Chapter relating to capital.

Article 53
Member States shall not introduce any new restrictions on the right of establishment in their territories of nationals of other Member States, save as otherwise provided in this Treaty.

Article 54
1. Before the end of the first stage, the Council shall, acting unanimously on a proposal from the Commission and after consulting the Economic and Social Committee and the European Parliament, draw up a general programme for the abolition of existing restrictions on freedom of

establishment within the Community. The Commission shall submit its proposal to the Council during the first two years of the first stage.

The programme shall set out the general conditions under which freedom of establishment is to be attained in the case of each type of activity and in particular the stages by which it is to be attained.

2. In order to implement this general programme or, in the absence of such programme, in order to achieve a stage in attaining freedom of establishment as regards a particular activity, the Council shall, acting on a proposal from the Commission, in co-operation with the European Parliament and after consulting the Economic and Social Committee, issue directives, acting unanimously until the end of the first stage and by a qualified majority thereafter.[1]

3. The Council and the Commission shall carry out the duties devolving upon them under the preceding provisions, in particular:

    (a)   by according, as a general rule, priority treatment to activities where freedom of establishment makes a particularly valuable contribution to the development of production and trade;

    (b)   by ensuring close co-operation between the competent authorities in the Member States in order to ascertain the particular situation within the Community of the various activities concerned;

    (c)   by abolishing those administrative procedures and practices, whether resulting from national legislation or from agreements previously concluded between Member States, the maintenance of which would form an obstacle to freedom of establishment;

    (d)   by ensuring that workers of one Member State employed in the territory of another Member State may remain in that territory for the purpose of taking up activities therein as self-employed persons, where they satisfy the conditions which they would be required to satisfy if they were entering that State at the time when they intended to take up such activities;

    (e)   by enabling a national of one Member State to acquire and use land and buildings situated in the territory of another Member State, in so far as this does not conflict with the principles laid down in Article 39 (2);

    (f)   by effecting the progressive abolition of restrictions on freedom of establishment in every branch of activity under consideration, both as regards the conditions for setting up agencies, branches or subsidiaries in the territory of a Member State and as regards the conditions governing the entry of personnel belonging to the main establishment into managerial or supervisory posts in such agencies, branches or subsidiaries;

    (g)   by co-ordinating to the necessary extent the safeguards which, for the protection of the interests of members and others, are required by Member States of companies or firms within the meaning of the second paragraph of Article 58 with a view to making such safeguards equivalent throughout the Community;

    (h)   by satisfying themselves that the conditions of establishment are not distorted by aids granted by Member States.

---

1 As amended by the Single European Act, arts 3 (1), 6 (4).

Article 55
The provisions of this Chapter shall not apply, so far as any given Member State is concerned, to activities which in that State are connected, even occasionally, with the exercise of official authority.

The Council may, acting by a qualified majority on a proposal from the Commission, rule that the provisions of this Chapter shall not apply to certain activities.

Article 56
1. The provisions of this Chapter and measures taken in pursuance thereof shall not prejudice the applicability of provisions laid down by law, regulation or administrative action providing for special treatment for foreign nationals on grounds of public policy, public security or public health.

2. Before the end of the transitional period, the Council shall, acting unanimously on a proposal from the Commission and after consulting the European Parliament, issue directives for the co-ordination of the aforementioned provisions laid down by law, regulation or administrative action. After the end of the second stage, however, the Council shall, acting by a qualified majority on a proposal from the Commission and in co-operation with the European Parliament, issue directives for the co-ordination of such provisions as, in each Member State, are a matter for regulation or administrative action.[1]

---

1 As amended by the Single European Act, art 6(5).

Article 57
1. In order to make it easier for persons to take up and pursue activities as self-employed persons, the Council shall, on a proposal from the Commission and in co-operation with the European Parliament, acting unanimously during the first stage and by a qualified majority thereafter, issue directives for the mutual recognition of diplomas, certificates and other evidence of formal qualifications.[1]

2. For the same purpose, the Council shall, before the end of the transitional period, acting on a proposal from the Commission and after consulting the European Parliament, issue directives for the co-ordination of the provisions laid down by law, regulation or administrative action in Member States concerning the taking up and pursuit of activities as self-employed persons. Unanimity shall be required for directives the implementation of which involves in at least one Member State amendment of the existing principles laid down by law governing the professions with respect to training and conditions of access for natural persons.[2] In other cases the Council shall act by a qualified majority, in co-operation with the European Parliament.[3]

3. In the case of the medical and allied and pharmaceutical professions, the progressive abolition of restrictions shall be dependent upon co-ordination of the conditions for their exercise in the various Member States.

---

1 As amended by Single European Act, art 6 (6).
2 As amended by Single European Act, art 16 (2).
3 As amended by Single European Act, art 6 (7).

Article 58
Companies or firms formed in accordance with the law of a Member State and having their registered office, central administration or principal place of business within the Community shall, for the purposes of this Chapter, be treated in the same way as natural persons who are nationals of Member States.

"Companies or firms" means companies or firms constituted under civil or commercial law, including cooperative societies, and other legal persons governed by public or private law, save for those which are non-profit-making.

CHAPTER 3-SERVICES

Article 59

Within the framework of the provisions set out below, restrictions on freedom to provide services within the Community shall be progressively abolished during the transitional period in respect of nationals of Member States who are established in a State of the Community other than that of the person for whom the services are intended.

The Council may, acting by a qualified majority on a proposal from the Commission, extend the provisions of this Chapter to nationals of a third country who provide services and who are established within the Community.[1]

_____

1 As amended by the Single European Act, art 16 (3).

Article 60

Services shall be considered to be "services" within the meaning of this Treaty where they are normally provided for remuneration, in so far as they are not governed by the provisions relating to freedom of movement for goods, capital and persons.

"Services" shall in particular include:
- (a)   activities of an industrial character;
- (b)   activities of a commercial character;
- (c)   activities of craftsmen;
- (d)   activities of the professions.

Without prejudice to the provisions of the Chapter relating to the right of establishment, the person providing a service may, in order to do so, temporarily pursue his activity in the State where the service is provided, under the same conditions as are imposed by that State on its own nationals.

Article 61

1. Freedom to provide services in the field of transport shall be governed by the provisions of the Title relating to transport.

2. The liberalisation of banking and insurance services connected with movements of capital shall be effected in step with the progressive liberalisation of movement of capital.

Article 62

Save as otherwise provided in this Treaty, Member States shall not introduce any new restrictions on the freedom to provide services which have in fact beenattained at the date of the entry into force of this Treaty.

Article 63

1. Before the end of the first stage, the Council shall, acting unanimously on a proposal from the Commission and after consulting the Economic and Social Committee and the European Parliament, draw up a general programme for the abolition of existing restrictions on freedom to provide services within the Community. The Commission shall submit its proposal to the Council during the first two years of the first stage.

The programme shall set out the general conditions under which and the stages by which each type of service is to be liberalised.

2. In order to implement this general programme or, in the absence of such programme, in order to achieve a stage in the liberalisation of a specific service, the Council shall, on a proposal from the Commission and after consulting the Economic and Social Committee and the European Parliament, issue directives, acting unanimously until the end of the first stage and by a qualified majority thereafter.

3. As regards the proposals and decisions referred to in paragraphs 1 and 2, priority shall as a general rule be given to those services which directly affect production costs or the liberalisation of which helps to promote trade in goods.

Article 64
The Member States declare their readiness to undertake the liberalisation of services beyond the extent required by the directives issued pursuant to Article 63 (2), if their general economic situation and the situation of the economic sector concerned so permit.

To this end, the Commission shall make recommendations to the Member States concerned.

Article 65
As long as restrictions on freedom to provide services have not been abolished, each Member State shall apply such restrictions without distinction on grounds of nationality or residence to all persons providing services within the meaning of the first paragraph of Article 59.

Article 66
The provisions of Articles 55 to 58 shall apply to the matters covered by this Chapter.

CHAPTER 4-CAPITAL

Article 67
1. During the transitional period and to the extent necessary to ensure the proper functioning of the common market, Member States shall progressively abolish between themselves all restrictions on the movement of capital belonging to persons resident in Member States and any discrimination based on the nationality or on the place of residence of the parties or on the place where such capital is invested.

2. Current payments connected with the movement of capital between Member States shall be freed from all restrictions by the end of the first stage at the latest.

Article 68
1. Member States shall, as regards the matters dealt with in this Chapter, be as liberal as possible in granting such exchange authorisations as are still necessary after the entry into force of this Treaty.

2. Where a Member State applies to the movements of capital liberalised in accordance with the provisions of this Chapter the domestic rules governing the capital market and the credit system, it shall do so in a non-discriminatory manner.

3. Loans for the direct or indirect financing of a Member State or its regional or local authorities shall not be issued or placed in other Member States unless the States concerned have reached agreement thereon. This provision shall

not preclude the application of Article 22 of the Protocol on the Statute of the European Investment Bank.

Article 69
The Council shall, on a proposal from the Commission, which for this purpose shall consult the Monetary Committee provided for in Article 105, issue the necessary directives for the progressive implementation of the provisions of Article 67, acting unanimously during the first two stages and by a qualified majority thereafter.

Article 70
1. The Commission shall propose to the Council measures for the progressive co-ordination of the exchange policies of Member States in respect of the movement of capital between those States and third countries. For this purpose the Council shall issue directives, acting by a qualified majority. It shall endeavour to attain the highest possible degree of liberalisation. Unanimity shall be required for measures which constitute a step back as regards the liberalisation of capital movements.[1]

2. Where the measures taken in accordance with paragraph 1 do not permit the elimination of differences between the exchange rules of Member States and where such differences could lead persons resident in one of the Member States to use the freer transfer facilities within the Community which are provided for in Article 67 in order to evade the rules of one of the Member States concerning the movement of capital to or from third countries, that State may, after consulting the other Member States and the Commission, take appropriate measures to overcome these difficulties.

Should the Council find that these measures are restricting the free movement of capital within the Community to a greater extent than is required for the purpose of overcoming the difficulties, it may, acting by a qualified majority on a proposal from the Commission, decide that the State concerned shall amend or abolish these measures.

---

1 As amended by the Single European Act, art 16 (4).

Article 71
Member States shall endeavour to avoid introducing within the Community any new exchange restrictions on the movement of capital and current payments connected with such movements, and shall endeavour not to make existing rules more restrictive.

They declare their readiness to go beyond the degree of liberalisation of capital movements provided for in the preceding Articles in so far as their economic situation, in particular the situation of their balance of payments, so permits.

The Commission may, after consulting the Monetary Committee, make recommendations to Member States on this subject.

Article 72
Member States shall keep the Commission informed of any movements of capital to and from third countries which come to their knowledge. The Commission may deliver to Member States any opinions which it considers appropriate on this subject.

Article 73
1. If movements of capital lead to disturbances in the functioning of the capital market in any Member State, the Commission shall, after consulting the Monetary Committee, authorise that State to take protective measures in the field of capital movements, the conditions and details of which the Commission shall determine.

The Council may, acting by a qualified majority, revoke this authorisation or amend the conditions or details thereof.

2. A Member State which is in difficulties may, however, on grounds of secrecy or urgency, take the measures mentioned above, where this proves necessary, on its own initiative. The Commission and the other Member States shall be informed of such measures by the date of their entry into force at the latest. In this event the Commission may, after consulting the Monetary Committee, decide that the State concerned shall amend or abolish the measures.

TITLE IV-TRANSPORT

Article 74
The objectives of this Treaty shall, in matters governed by this Title, be pursued by Member States within the framework of a common transport policy.

Article 75
1. For the purpose of implementing Article 74, and taking into account the distinctive features of transport, the Council shall, acting unanimously until the end of the second stage and by a qualified majority thereafter, lay down, on a proposal from the Commission and after consulting the Economic and Social Committee and the European Parliament :
  (a)   common rules applicable to international transport to or from the territory of a Member State or passing across the territory of one or more Member States;
  (b)   the conditions under which non-resident carriers may operate transport services within a Member State;
  (c)   any other appropriate provisions.

2. The provisions referred to in (a) and (b) of paragraph 1 shall be laid down during the transitional period.

3. By way of derogation from the procedure provided for in paragraph 1, where the application of provisions concerning the principles of the regulatory system for transport would be liable to have a serious effect on the standard of living and on employment in certain areas and on the operation of transport facilities, they shall be laid down by the Council acting unanimously. In so doing, the Council shall take into account the need for adaptation to the economic development which will result from establishing the common market.

Article 76
Until the provisions referred to in Article 75 (1) have been laid down, no Member State may, without the unanimous approval of the Council, make the various provisions governing the subject when this Treaty enters into force less favourable in their direct or indirect effect on carriers of other Member States as compared with carriers who are nationals of that State.

Article 77
Aids shall be compatible with this Treaty if they meet the needs of co-ordination of transport or if they represent re-imbursement for the discharge of certain obligations inherent in the concept of a public service.

Article 78
Any measures taken within the framework of this Treaty in respect of transport rates and conditions shall take account of the economic circumstances of carriers.

Article 79

1. In the case of transport within the Community, discrimination which takes the form of carriers charging different rates and imposing different conditions for the carriage of the same goods over the same transport links on grounds of the country of origin or of destination of the goods in question, shall be abolished, at the latest, before the end of the second stage.

2. Paragraph 1 shall not prevent the Council from adopting other measures in pursuance of Article 75 (1).

3. Within two years of the entry into force of this Treaty, the Council shall, acting by a qualified majority on a proposal from the Commission and after consulting the Economic and Social Committee, lay down rules for implementing the provisions of paragraph 1.

The Council may in particular lay down the provisions needed to enable the institutions of the Community to secure compliance with the rule laid down in paragraph 1 and to ensure that users benefit from it to the full.

4. The Commission shall, acting on its own initiative or on application by a Member State, investigate any cases of discrimination falling within paragraph 1 and, after consulting any Member State concerned, shall take the necessary decisions within the framework of the rules laid down in accordance with the provisions of paragraph 3.

Article 80

1. The imposition by a Member State, in respect of transport operations carried out within the Community, of rates and conditions involving any element of support or protection in the interest of one or more particular undertakings or industries shall be prohibited as from the beginning of the second stage, unless authorised by the Commission.

2. The Commission shall, acting on its own initiative or on application by a Member State, examine the rates and conditions referred to in paragraph 1 taking account in particular of the requirements of an appropriate regional economic policy, the needs of underdeveloped areas and the problems of areas seriously affected by political circumstances on the one hand, and of the effects of such rates and conditions on competition between the different modes of transport on the other.

After consulting each Member State concerned, the Commission shall take the necessary decisions.

3. The prohibition provided for in paragraph 1 shall not apply to tariffs fixed to meet competition.

Article 81

Charges or dues in respect of the crossing of frontiers which are charged by a carrier in addition to the transport rates shall not exceed a reasonable level after taking the costs actually incurred thereby into account.

Member States shall endeavour to reduce these costs progressively.

The Commission may make recommendations to Member States for the application of this Article.

Article 82

The provisions of this Title shall not form an obstacle to the application of measures taken in the Federal Republic of Germany to the extent that such measures are required in order to compensate for the economic disadvantages caused by the division of Germany to the economy of certain areas of the Federal Republic affected by that division.

Article 83

An Advisory Committee consisting of experts designated by the Governments of Member States, shall be attached to the Commission. The Commission, whenever it considers it desirable, shall consult the Committee on transport matters without prejudice to the powers of the transport section of the Economic and Social Committee.

Article 84

1. The provisions of this Title shall apply to transport by rail, road and inland waterway.

2. The Council may, acting by a qualified majority, decide whether, to what extent and by what procedure appropriate provisions may be laid down for sea and air transport.

The procedural provisions of Article 75 (1) and (3) shall apply.[1]

---

1 As amended by the Single European Act, art 16 (5), (6).

PART THREE

POLICY OF THE COMMUNITY

TITLE I
COMMON RULES

CHAPTER 1-RULES ON COMPETITION

Section 1-Rules applying to undertakings

Article 85

1. The following shall be prohibited as incompatible with the common market: all agreements between undertakings, decisions by associations of undertakings and concerted practices which may affect trade between Member States and which have as their object or effect the prevention, restriction or distortion of competition within the common market, and in particular those which:

 (a) directly or indirectly fix purchase or selling prices or any other trading conditions;

 (b) limit or control production, markets, technical development, or investment;

 (c) share markets or sources of supply;

 (d) apply dissimilar conditions to equivalent transactions with other trading parties, thereby placing them at a competitive disadvantage;

 (e) make the conclusion of contracts subject to acceptance by the other parties of supplementary obligations which, by their nature or according to commercial usage, have no connection with the subject of such contracts.

2. Any agreements or decisions prohibited pursuant to this Article shall be automatically void.

3. The provisions of paragraph 1 may, however, be declared inapplicable in the case of:

 - any agreement or category of agreements between undertakings;

 - any decision or category of decisions by associations of undertakings;

 - any concerted practice or category of concerted practices;

which contributes to improving the production or distribution of goods or to

155

promoting technical or economic progress while allowing consumers a fair share of the resulting benefit, and which does not:

(a)   impose on the undertakings concerned restrictions which are not indispensable to the attainment of these objectives;

(b)   afford such undertakings the possibility of eliminating competition in respect of a substantial part of the products in question.

Article 86

Any abuse by one or more undertakings of a dominant position within the common market or in a substantial part of it shall be prohibited as incompatible with the common market in so far as it may affect trade between Member States.

Such abuse may, in particular, consist in:

(a)   directly or indirectly imposing unfair purchase or selling prices or other unfair trading conditions;

(b)   limiting production, markets or technical development to the prejudice of consumers;

(c)   applying dissimilar conditions to equivalent transactions with other trading parties, thereby placing them at a competitive disadvantage;

(d)   making the conclusion of contracts subject to acceptance by the other parties of supplementary obligations which, by their nature or according to commercial usage, have no connection with the subject of such contracts.

Article 87

1. Within three years of the entry into force of this Treaty the Council shall, acting unanimously on a proposal from the Commission and after consulting the European Parliament, adopt any appropriate regulations or directives to give effect to the principles set out in Articles 85 and 86.

If such provisions have not been adopted within the period mentioned, they shall be laid down by the Council, acting by a qualified majority on a proposal from the Commission and after consulting the European Parliament.

2. The regulations or directives referred to in paragraph 1 shall be designed in particular:

(a)   to ensure compliance with the prohibitions laid down in Article 85 (1) and in Article 86 by making provision for fines and periodic penalty payments;

(b)   to lay down detailed rules for the application of Article 85 (3), taking into account the need to ensure effective supervision on the one hand, and to simplify administration to the greatest possible extent on the other;

(c)   to define, if need be, in the various branches of the economy, the scope of the provisions of Articles 85 and 86;

(d)   to define the respective functions of the Commission and of the Court of Justice in applying the provisions laid down in this paragraph;

(e)   to determine the relationship between national laws and the provisions contained in this Section or adopted pursuant to this Article.

Article 88

Until the entry into force of the provisions adopted in pursuance of Article 87, the authorities in Member States shall rule on the admissibility of agreements, decisions and concerted practices and on abuse of a dominant position in the common market in accordance with the law of their country and with the provisions of Article 85, in particular paragraph 3, and of Article 86.

Article 89

1. Without prejudice to Article 88, the Commission shall, as soon as it takes up its duties, ensure the application of the principles laid down in Articles 85 and 86. On application by a Member State or on its own initiative, and in co-operation with the competent authorities in the Member States, who shall give it their assistance, the Commission shall investigate cases of suspected infringement of these principles. If it finds that there has been an infringement, it shall propose appropriate measures to bring it to an end.

2. If the infringement is not brought to an end, the Commission shall record such infringement of the principles in a reasoned decision. The Commission may publish its decision and authorise Member States to take the measures, the conditions and details of which it shall determine, needed to remedy the situation.

Article 90

1. In the case of public undertakings and undertakings to which Member States grant special or exclusive rights, Member States shall neither enact nor maintain in force any measure contrary to the rules contained in this Treaty, in particular those rules provided for in Article 7 and Articles 85 to 94.

2. Undertakings entrusted with the operation of services of general economic interest or having the character of a revenue-producing monopoly shall be subject to the rules contained in this Treaty, in particular to the rules on competition, in so far as the application of such rules does not obstruct the performance, in law or in fact, of the particular tasks assigned to them. The development of trade must not be affected to such an extent as would be contrary to the interests of the Community.

3. The Commission shall ensure the application of the provisions of this Article and shall, where necessary, address appropriate directives or decisions to Member States.

Section 2-Dumping

Article 91

1. If during the transitional period, the Commission, on application by a Member State or by any other interested party, finds that dumping is being practised within the common market, it shall address recommendations to the person or persons with whom such practices originate for the purpose of putting an end to them.

Should the practices continue, the Commission shall authorise the injured Member State to take protective measures, the conditions and details of which the Commission shall determine.

2. As soon as this Treaty enters into force, products which originate in or are in free circulation in one Member State and which have been exported to another Member State shall, on reimportation, be admitted into the territory of the first-mentioned State free of all customs duties, quantitative restrictions or measures having equivalent effect. The Commission shall lay down appropriate rules for the application of this paragraph.

Section 3-Aids granted by States

Article 92

1. Save as otherwise provided in this Treaty, any aid granted by a Member State or through State resources in any form whatsoever which distorts or threatens to distort competition by favouring certain undertakings or the production of certain goods shall, in so far as it affects trade between Member States, be incompatible with the common market.

2. The following shall be compatible with the common market:
- (a)   aid having a social character, granted to individual consumers, provided that such aid is granted without discrimination related to the origin of the products concerned;
- (b)   aid to make good the damage caused by natural disasters or exceptional occurrences;
- (c)   aid granted to the economy of certain areas of the Federal Republic of Germany affected by the division of Germany in so far as such aid is required in order to compensate for the economic disadvantages caused by that division.

3. The following may be considered to be compatible with the common market:
- (a)   aid to promote the economic development of areas where the standard of living is abnormally low or where there is serious under-employment;
- (b)   aid to promote the execution of an important project of common European interest or to remedy a serious disturbance in the economy of a Member State;
- (c)   aid to facilitate the development of certain economic activities or of certain economic areas, where such aid does not adversely affect trading conditions to an extent contrary to the common interest. However, the aids granted to ship building as of 1 January 1957 shall, in so far as they serve only to compensate for the absence of customs protection, be progressively reduced under the same conditions as apply to the elimination of customs duties, subject to the provisions of this Treaty concerning common commercial policy towards third countries;
- (d)   such other categories of aid as may be specified by decision of the Council acting by a qualified majority on a proposal from the Commission.

Article 93
1. The Commission shall, in co-operation with Member States, keep under constant review all systems of aid existing in those States. It shall propose to the latter any appropriate measures required by the progressive development or by the functioning of the common market.

2. If, after giving notice to the parties concerned to submit their comments, the Commission finds that aid granted by a State or through State resources is not compatible with the common market having regard to Article 92, or that such aid is being misused, it shall decide that the State concerned shall abolish or alter such aid within a period of time to be determined by the Commission.

If the State concerned does not comply with this decision within the pre-scribed time, the Commission or any other interested State may, in derogation from the provisions of Articles 169 and 170, refer the matter to the Court of Justice direct.

On application by a Member State, the Council, may, acting unanimously, decide that aid which that State is granting or intends to grant shall be considered to be compatible with the common market, in derogation from the provisions of Article 92 or from the regulations provided for in Article 94, if such a decision is justified by exceptional circumstances. If, as regards the aid in question, the Commission has already initiated the procedure provided for in the first sub-paragraph of this paragraph, the fact that the State concerned has made its application to the Council shall have the effect of suspending that procedure until the Council has made its attitude known.

If, however, the Council has not made its attitude known within three months

of the said application being made, the Commission shall give its decision on the case.

3. The Commission shall be informed, in sufficient time to enable it to submit its comments, of any plans to grant or alter aid. If it considers that any such plan is not compatible with the common market having regard to Article 92, it shall without delay initiate the procedure provided for in paragraph 2. The Member State concerned shall not put its proposed measures into effect until this procedure has resulted in a final decision.

Article 94
The Council may, acting by a qualified majority on a proposal from the Commission, make any appropriate regulations for the application of Articles 92 and 93 and may in particular determine the conditions in which Article 93(3) shall apply and the categories of aid exempted from this procedure.

CHAPTER 2-TAX PROVISIONS

Article 95
No Member State shall impose, directly or indirectly, on the products of other Member States any internal taxation of any kind in excess of that imposed directly or indirectly on similar domestic products.

Furthermore, no Member State shall impose on the products of other Member States any internal taxation of such a nature as to afford indirect protection to other products.

Member States shall, not later than at the beginning of the second stage, repeal or amend any provisions existing when this Treaty enters into force which conflict with the preceding rules.

Article 96
Where products are exported to the territory of any Member State, any repayment of internal taxation shall not exceed the internal taxation imposed on them, whether directly or indirectly.

Article 97
Member States which levy a turnover tax calculated on a cumulative multistage tax system may, in the case of internal taxation imposed by them on imported products or of repayments allowed by them on exported products, establish average rates for products or groups of products, provided that there is no infringement of the principles laid down in Articles 95 and 96.

Where the average rates established by a Member State do not conform to these principles, the Commission shall address appropriate directives or decisions to the State concerned.

Article 98
In the case of charges other than turnover taxes, excise duties and other forms of indirect taxation, remissions and repayments in respect of exports to other Member States may not be granted and countervailing charges in respect of imports from Member States may not be imposed unless the measures contemplated have been previously approved for a limited period by the Council acting by a qualified majority on a proposal from the Commission.

Article 99
The Council shall, acting unanimously on a proposal from the Commission and after consulting the European Parliament, adopt provisions for the harmonisation of legislation concerning turnover taxes, excise duties and

other forms of indirect taxation to the extent that such harmonisation is necessary to ensure the establishment and the functioning of the internal market within the time-limit laid down in Article 8a.[1]

1 Substituted by the Single European Act, art 17.

CHAPTER 3-APPROXIMATION OF LAWS

Article 100

The Council shall, acting unanimously on a proposal from the Commission, issue directives for the approximation of such provisions laid down by law, regulation or administrative action in Member States as directly affect the establishment or functioning of the common market.

The European Parliament and the Economic and Social Committee shall be consulted in the case of directives whose implementation would, in one or more Member States, involve the amendment of legislation.

Article 100A[1]

1. By way of derogation from Article 100 and save where otherwise provided in this Treaty, the following provisions shall apply for the achievement of the objectives set out in Article 8a. The Council shall, acting by a qualified majority on a proposal from the Commission in co-operation with the European Parliament and after consulting the Economic and Social Committee, adopt the measures for the approximation of the provisions laid down by law, regulation or administrative action in Member States which have as their object the establishment and functioning of the internal market.

2. Paragraph 1 shall not apply to fiscal provisions, to those relating to the free movement of persons nor to those relating to the rights and interests of employed persons.

3. The Commission, in its proposals envisaged in paragraph 1 concerning health, safety, environmental protection and consumer protection, will take as a base a high level of protection.

4. If, after the adoption of a harmonisation measure by the Council acting by a qualified majority, a Member State deems it necessary to apply national provisions on grounds of major needs referred to in Article 36, or relating to protection of the environment or the working environment, it shall notify the Commission of these provisions.

The Commission shall confirm the provisions involved after having verified that they are not a means of arbitrary discrimination or a disguised restriction on trade between Member States.

By way of derogation from the procedure laid down in Articles 169 and 170, the Commission or any Member State may bring the matter directly before the Court of Justice if it considers that another Member State is making improper use of the powers provided for in this Article.

5. The harmonisation measures referred to above shall, in appropriate cases, include a safeguard clause authorising the Member States to take, for one or more of the non-economic reasons referred to in Article 36, provisional measures subject to a Community control procedure.

1 Added by the Single European Act, art 18.

Article 100B[1]

1. During 1992, the Commission shall, together with each Member State, draw up an inventory of national laws, regulations and administrative provisions which fall under Article 100a and which have not been harmonised pursuant to that Article.

The Council, acting in accordance with the provisions of Article 100a, may decide that the provisions in force in a Member State must be recognised as being equivalent to those applied by another Member State.

2. The provisions of Article 100a (4) shall apply by analogy.

3. The Commission shall draw up the inventory referred to in the first subparagraph of paragraph 1 and shall submit appropriate proposals in good time to allow the Council to act before the end of 1992.

1 Added by the Single European Act, art 19.

Article 101

Where the Commission finds that a difference between the provisions laid down by law, regulation or administrative action in Member States is distorting the conditions of competition in the common market and that the resultant distortion needs to be eliminated, it shall consult the Member States concerned.

If such consultation does not result in an agreement eliminating the distortion in question, the Council shall, on a proposal from the Commission, acting unanimously during the first stage and by a qualified majority thereafter, issue the necessary directives. The Commission and the Council may take any other appropriate measures provided for in this Treaty.

Article 102

1. Where there is reason to fear that the adoption or amendment of a provision laid down by law, regulation or administrative action may cause distortion within the meaning of Article 101, a Member State desiring to proceed therewith shall consult the Commission. After consulting the Member States, the Commission shall recommend to the States concerned such measures as may be appropriate to avoid the distortion in question.

2. If a State desiring to introduce or amend its own provisions does not comply with the recommendation addressed to it b), the Commission, other Member States shall not be required, in pursuance of Article 101, to amend their own provisions in order to eliminate such distortion. If the Member State which has ignored the recommendation of the Commission causes distortion detrimental only to itself, the provisions of Article 101 shall not apply.

TITLE II
ECONOMIC POLICY

CHAPTER 1-CO-OPERATION IN ECONOMIC AND MONETARY POLICY
(ECONOMIC AND MONETARY UNION) [1]

1 Chapter added by the Single European Act, Art 20.

Article 102a

1. In order to ensure the convergence of economic and monetary policies which is necessary for the further development of the Community, Member States shall co-operate in accordance with the objectives of Article 104. In so

doing, they shall take account of the experience acquired in cooperation within the framework of the European Monetary System (EMS) and in developing the ECU, and shall respect existing powers in this field.

2. In so far as further development in the field of economic and monetary policy necessitates institutional changes, the provisions of Article 236 shall be applicable. The Monetary Committee and the Committee of Governors of the Central Banks shall also be consulted regarding institutional changes in the monetary area.

CHAPTER 2-CONJUNCTURAL POLICY[1]

1 Renumbering of Chapter by the Single European Act, Art 20 (2).

Article 103
1. Member States shall regard their conjunctural policies as a matter of common concern. They shall consult each other and the Commission on the measures to be taken in the light of the prevailing circumstances.

2. Without prejudice to any other procedures provided for in this Treaty, the Council may, acting unanimously on a proposal from the Commission, decide upon the measures appropriate to the situation.

3. Acting by a qualified majority on a proposal from the Commission, the Council shall, where required, issue any directives needed to give effect to the measures decided upon under paragraph 2.

4. The procedures provided for in this Article shall also apply if any difficulty should arise in the supply of certain products.

CHAPTER 3-BALANCE OF PAYMENTS[1]

1 Renumbering of Chapter by the Single European Act, Art 20 (2).

Article 104
Each Member State shall pursue the economic policy needed to ensure the equilibrium of its overall balance of payments and to maintain confidence in its currency, while taking care to ensure a high level of employment and a stable level of prices.

Article 105
1. In order to facilitate attainment of the objectives set out in Article 104, Member States shall co-ordinate their economic policies. They shall for this purpose provide for co-operation between their appropriate administrative departments and between their central banks.

The Commission shall submit to the Council recommendations on how to achieve such co-operation.

2. In order to promote co-ordination of the policies of Member States in the monetary field to the full extent needed for the functioning of the common market, a Monetary Committee with advisory status is hereby set up. It shall have the following tasks:
    - to keep under review the monetary and financial situation of the Member States and of the Community and the general payments system of the Member States and to report regularly thereon to the Council and to the Commission;
    - to deliver opinions at the request of the Council or of the Commission or on its own initiative, for submission to these institutions.

The Member States and the Commission shall each appoint two members of the Monetary Committee.

Article 106

1. Each Member State undertakes to authorise, in the currency of the Member State in which the creditor or the beneficiary resides, any payments connected with the movement of goods, services or capital, and any transfers of capital and earnings, to the extent that the movement of goods, services, capital and persons between Member States has been liberalised pursuant to this Treaty.

The Member States declare their readiness to undertake the liberalisation of payments beyond the extent provided in the preceding sub-paragraph, in so far as their economic situation in general and the state of their balance of payments in particular so permit.

2. In so far as movements of goods, services, and capital are limited only by restrictions on payments connected therewith, these restrictions shall be progressively abolished by applying, *mutatis mutandis*, the provisions of the Chapters relating to the abolition of quantitative restrictions, to the liberalisation of services and to the free movement of capital.

3. Member States undertake not to introduce between themselves any new restrictions on transfers connected with the invisible transactions listed in Annex III to this Treaty.

The progressive abolition of existing restrictions shall be effected in accordance with the provisions of Articles 63 to 65, in so far as such abolition is not governed by the provisions contained in paragraphs 1 and 2 or by the Chapter relating to the free movement of capital.

4. If need be, Member States shall consult each other on the measures to be taken to enable the payments and transfers mentioned in this Article to be effected; such measures shall not prejudice the attainment of the objectives set out in this Chapter.

Article 107

1. Each Member State shall treat its policy with regard to rates of exchange as a matter of common concern.

2. If a Member State makes an alteration in its rate of exchange which is inconsistent with the objectives set out in Article 104 and which seriously distorts conditions of competition, the Commission may, after consulting the Monetary Committee, authorise other Member States to take for a strictly limited period the necessary measures, the conditions and details of which it shall determine, in order to counter the consequences of such alteration.

Article 108

1. Where a Member State is in difficulties or is seriously threatened with difficulties as regards its balance of payments either as a result of an overall disequilibrium in its balance of payments, or as a result of the type of currency at its disposal, and where such difficulties are liable in particular to jeopardise the functioning of the common market or the progressive implementation of the common commercial policy, the Commission shall immediately investigate the position of the State in question and the action which, making use of all the means at its disposal, that State has taken or may take in accordance with the provisions of Article 104. The Commission shall state what measures it recommends the State concerned to take.

If the action taken by a Member State and the measures suggested by the Commission do not prove sufficient to overcome the difficulties which have arisen or which threaten, the Commission shall, after consulting the Monetary

Committee, recommend to the Council the granting of mutual assistance and appropriate methods therefor.

The Commission shall keep the Council regularly informed of the situation and of how it is developing.

2. The Council, acting by a qualified majority, shall grant such mutual assistance; it shall adopt directives or decisions laying down the condition and details of such assistance, which may take such forms as:

(a) a concerted approach to or within any other international organisations to which Member States may have recourse;

(b) measures needed to avoid deflection of trade where the State which is in difficulties maintains or reintroduces quantitative restrictions against third countries;

(c) the granting of limited credits by other Member States, subject to their agreement.

During the transitional period, mutual assistance may also take the form of special reductions in customs duties or enlargements of quotas in order to facilitate an increase in imports from the State which is in difficulties, subject to the agreement of the States by which such measures would have to be taken.

3. If the mutual assistance recommended by the Commission is not granted by the Council or if the mutual assistance granted and the measures taken are insufficient, the Commission shall authorise the State which is in difficulties to take protective measures, the conditions and details of which the Commission shall determine.

Such authorisation may be revoked and such conditions and details may be changed by the Council acting by a qualified majority.

Article 109

1. Where a sudden crisis in the balance of payments occurs and a decision within the meaning of Article 108 (2) is not immediately taken, the Member State concerned may, as a precaution, take the necessary protective measures. Such measures must cause the least possible disturbance in the functioning of the common market and must not be wider in scope than is strictly necessary to remedy the sudden difficulties which have arisen.

2. The Commission and the other Member States shall be informed of such protective measures not later than when they enter into force. The Commission may recommend to the Council the granting of mutual assistance under Article 108.

3. After the Commission has delivered an opinion and the Monetary Committee has been consulted, the Council may, acting by a qualified majority, decide that the State concerned shall amend, suspend or abolish the protective measures referred to above.

CHAPTER 4-COMMERCIAL POLICY[1]

1 Renumbering of Chapter by the Single European Act, Art 20 (2).

Article 110

By establishing a customs union between themselves Member States aim to contribute, in the common interest, to the harmonious development of world trade, the progressive abolition of restrictions on international trade and the lowering of customs barriers.

The common commercial policy shall take into account the favourable effect which the abolition of customs duties between Member States may have on the increase in the competitive strength of undertakings in those States.

Article 111
The following provisions shall, without prejudice to Articles 115 and 116, apply during the transitional period:

1. Member States shall co-ordinate their trade relations with third countries so as to bring about, by the end of the transitional period, the conditions needed for implementing a common policy in the field of external trade.

The Commission shall submit to the Council proposals regarding the procedure for common action to be followed during the transitional period and regarding the achievement of uniformity in their commercial policies.

2. The Commission shall submit to the Council recommendations for tariff negotiations with third countries in respect of the common customs tariff.

The Council shall authorise the Commission to open such negotiations.

The Commission shall conduct these negotiations in consultation with a special committee appointed by the Council to assist the Commission in this task and within the framework of such directives as the Council may issue to it.

3. In exercising the powers conferred upon it by this Article, the Council shall act unanimously during the first two stages and by a qualified majority thereafter.

4. Member States shall, in consultation with the Commission, take all necessary measures, particularly those designed to bring about an adjustment of tariff agreements in force with third countries, in order that the entry into force of the common customs tariff shall not be delayed.

5. Member States shall aim at securing as high a level of uniformity as possible between themselves as regards their liberalisation lists in relation to third countries or groups of third countries. To this end, the Commission shall make all appropriate recommendations to Member States.

If Member States abolish or reduce quantitative restrictions in relation to third countries, they shall inform the Commission beforehand and shall accord the same treatment to other Member States.

Article 112
1. Without prejudice to obligations undertaken by them within the framework of other international organisations, Member States shall, before the end of the transitional period, progressively harmonise the systems whereby they grant aid for exports to third countries, to the extent necessary to ensure that competition between undertakings of the Community is not distorted.

On a proposal from the Commission, the Council, shall, acting unanimously until the end of the second stage and by a qualified majority thereafter, issue any directives needed for this purpose.

2. The preceding provisions shall not apply to such drawback of customs duties or charges having equivalent effect nor to such repayment of indirect taxation including turnover taxes, excise duties and other indirect taxes as is allowed when goods are exported from a Member State to a third country, in so far as such drawback or repayment does not exceed the amount imposed, directly or indirectly, on the products exported.

Article 113

1. After the transitional period has ended, the common commercial policy shall be based on uniform principles, particularly in regard to changes in tariff rates, the conclusion of tariff and trade agreements, the achievement of uniformity in measures of liberalisation, export policy and measures to protect trade such as those to be taken in case of dumping or subsidies.

2. The Commission shall submit proposals to the Council for implementing the common commercial policy.

3. Where agreements with third countries need to be negotiated, the Commission shall make recommendations to the Council, which shall authorise the Commission to open the necessary negotiations.

The Commission shall conduct these negotiations in consultation with a special committee appointed by the Council to assist the Commission in this task and within the framework of such directives as the Council may issue to it.

4. In exercising the powers conferred upon it by this Article, the Council shall act by a qualified majority.

Article 114

The agreements referred to in Article 111 (2) and in Article 113 shall be concluded by the Council on behalf of the Community, acting unanimously during the first two stages and by a qualified majority thereafter.

Article 115

In order to ensure that the execution of measures of commercial policy taken in accordance with this Treaty by any Member State is not obstructed by deflection of trade, or where differences between such measures lead to economic difficulties in one or more of the Member States, the Commission shall recommend the methods for the requisite co-operation between Member States. Failing this, the Commission shall authorise Member States to take the necessary protective measures, the conditions and details of which it shall determine.

In case of urgency during the transitional period, Member States may themselves take the necessary measures and shall notify them to the other Member States and to the Commission, which may decide that the States concerned shall amend or abolish such measures.

In the selection of such measures, priority shall be given to those which cause the least disturbance to the functioning of the common market and which take into account the need to expedite, as far as possible, the introduction of the common customs tariff.

Article 116

From the end of the transitional period onwards, Member States shall, in respect of all matters of particular interest to the common market, proceed within the framework of international organisations of an economic character only by common action. To this end, the Commission shall submit to the Council, which shall act by a qualified majority, proposals concerning the scope and implementation of such common action.

During the transitional period, Member States shall consult each other for the purpose of concerting the action they take and adopting as far as possible a uniform attitude.

TITLE III
SOCIAL POLICY

CHAPTER 1-SOCIAL PROVISIONS

Article 117
Member States agree upon the need to promote improved working conditions and an improved standard of living for workers, so as to make possible their harmonisation while the improvement is being maintained.

They believe that such a development will ensue not only from the functioning of the common market, which will favour the harmonisation of social systems, but also from the procedures provided for in this Treaty and from the approximation of provisions laid down by law, regulation or administrative action.

Article 118
Without prejudice to the other provisions of this Treaty and in conformity with its general objectives, the Commission shall have the task of promoting close co-operation between Member States in the social field, particularly in matters relating to:
- employment;
- labour law and working conditions;
- basic and advanced vocational training;
- social security;
- prevention of occupational accidents and diseases;
- occupational hygiene;
- the right of association, and collective bargaining between employers and workers.

To this end, the Commission shall act in close contact with Member States by making studies, delivering opinions and arranging consultations both on problems arising at national level and on those of concern to international organisations.

Before delivering the opinions provided for in this Article, the Commission shall consult the Economic and Social Committee.

Article 118a [1]
1. Member States shall pay particular attention to encouraging improvements, especially in the working environment, as regards the health and safety of workers, and shall set as their objective the harmonisation of conditions in this area, while maintaining the improvements made.

2. In order to help achieve the objective laid down in the first paragraph, the Council, acting by a qualified majority on a proposal from the Commission, in co-operation with the European Parliament and after consulting the Economic and Social Committee, shall adopt, by means of directives, minimum requirements for gradual implementation, having regard to the conditions and technical rules obtaining in each of the Member States.

Such directives shall avoid imposing administrative, financial and legal constraints in a way which would hold back the creation and development of small and medium-sized undertakings.

3. The provisions adopted pursuant to this Article shall not prevent any Member State from maintaining or introducing more stringent measures for the protection of working conditions compatible with this Treaty.

---

1 As added by the Single European Act, art 21.

Article 118b[1]

The Commission shall endeavour to develop the dialogue between management and labour at European level which could, if the two sides consider it desirable, lead to relations based on agreement.

1 As added by the Single European Act, art 22.

Article 119

Each Member State shall during the first stage ensure and subsequently maintain the application of the principle that men and women should receive equal pay for equal work.

For the purpose of this Article, "pay" means the ordinary basic or minimum wage or salary and any other consideration, whether in cash or in kind, which the worker receives, directly or indirectly, in respect of his employment from his employer.

Equal pay without discrimination based on sex means:
    (a)   that pay for the same work at piece rates shall be calculated on the basis of the same unit of measurement;
    (b)   that pay for work at time rates shall be the same for the same job.

Article 120

Member States shall endeavour to maintain the existing equivalence between paid holiday schemes.

Article 121

The Council may, acting unanimously and after consulting the Economic and Social Committee, assign to the Commission tasks in connection with the implementation of common measures, particularly as regards social security for the migrant workers referred to in Articles 48 to 51.

Article 122

The Commission shall include a separate chapter on social developments within the Community in its annual report to the European Parliament.

The European Parliament may invite the Commission to draw up reports on any particular problems concerning social conditions.

CHAPTER 2-THE EUROPEAN SOCIAL FUND

Article 123

In order to improve employment opportunities for workers in the common market and to contribute thereby to raising the standard of living, a European Social Fund is hereby established in accordance with the provisions set out below; it shall have the task of rendering the employment of workers easier and of increasing their geographical and occupational mobility within the Community.

Article 124

The Fund shall be administered by the Commission.

The Commission shall be assisted in this task by a Committee presided over by a member of the Commission and composed of representatives of Governments, trade unions and employers' organisations.

Article 125

1. On application by a Member State the Fund shall, within the framework of the rules provided for in Article 127, meet 50% of the expenditure incurred after the entry into force of this Treaty by that State or by a body governed by

public law for the purposes of:

  (a)   ensuring productive re-employment of workers by means of:
          - vocational retraining;
          - resettlement allowances;
  (b)   granting aid for the benefit of workers whose employment is
          reduced or temporarily suspended, in whole or in part, as a
          result of the conversion of an undertaking to other
          production, in order that they may retain the same wage level
          pending their full re-employment.

2. Assistance granted by the Fund towards the cost of vocational retraining
shall be granted only if the unemployed workers could not be found
employment except in a new occupation and only if they have been in
productive employment for at least six months in the occupation for which
they have been retrained.

Assistance towards resettlement allowances shall be granted only if the
unemployed workers have been caused to change their home within the
Community and have been in productive employment for at least six months
in their new place of residence.

Assistance for workers in the case of the conversion of an undertaking shall
be granted only if:

  (a)   the workers concerned have again been fully employed in
          that undertaking for at least six months;
  (b)   the Government concerned has submitted a plan beforehand,
          drawn up by the undertaking in question, for that particular
          conversion and for financing it;
  (c)   the Commission has given its prior approval to the
          conversion plan.

Article 126

When the transitional period has ended, the Council, after receiving the
opinion of the Commission and after consulting the Economic and Social
Committee and the European Parliament, may:

  (a)   rule, by a qualified majority, that all or part of the assistance
          referred to in Article 125 shall no longer be granted; or
  (b)   unanimously determine what new tasks may be entrusted to
          the Fund within the framework of its terms of reference as
          laid down in Article 123.

Article 127

The Council shall, acting by a qualified majority on a proposal from the
Commission and after consulting the Economic and Social Committee and the
European Parliament, lay down the provisions required to implement
Articles 124 to 126; in particular it shall determine in detail the conditions
under which assistance shall be granted by the Fund in accordance with
Article 125 and the classes of undertakings whose workers
shall benefit from the assistance provided for in Article 125 (1)(b).

Article 128

The Council shall, acting on a proposal from the Commission and after
consulting the Economic and Social Committee, lay down general principles
for implementing a common vocational training policy capable of
contributing to the harmonious development both of the national economies
and of the common market.

TITLE IV
THE EUROPEAN INVESTMENT BANK

Article 129
A European Investment Bank is hereby established; it shall have legal personality.

The members of the European Investment Bank shall be the Member States.

The Statute of the European Investment Bank is laid down in a Protocol annexed to this Treaty.

Article 130
The task of the European Investment Bank shall be to contribute, by having recourse to the capital market and utilising its own resources, to the balanced and steady development of the common market in the interest of the Community. For this purpose the Bank shall, operating on a non-profit-making basis, grant loans and give guarantees which facilitate the financing of the following projects in all sectors of the economy:

    (a)   projects for developing less-developed regions;

    (b)   projects for modernising or converting undertakings or for developing fresh activities called for by the progressive establishment of the common market, where these projects are of such a size or nature that they cannot be entirely financed by the various means available in the individual Member States;

    (c)   projects of common interest to several Member States which are of such a size or nature that they cannot be entirely financed by the various means available in the individual Member States.

TITLE V
ECONOMIC AND SOCIAL COHESION[1]

1 Title V and Articles therein added by the Single European Act, art 23.

Article 130a
In order to promote its overall harmonious development, the Community shall develop and pursue its actions leading to the strengthening of its economic and social cohesion.

In particular the Community shall aim at reducing disparities between the various regions and the backwardness of the least-favoured regions.

Article 130b
Member States shall conduct their economic policies, and shall co-ordinate them, in such a way as, in addition, to attain the objectives set out in Article 130a. The implementation of the common policies and of the internal market shall take into account the objectives set out in Article 130a and in Article 130c and shall contribute to their achievement. The Community shall support the achievement of these objectives by the action it takes through the structural Funds (European Agricultural Guidance and Guarantee Fund, Guidance Section, European Social Fund, European Regional Development Fund), the European Investment Bank and the other existing financial instruments.

Article 130c
The European Regional Development Fund is intended to help redress the

principal regional imbalances in the Community through participating in the development and structural adjustment of regions whose development is lagging behind and in the conversion of declining industrial regions.

Article 130d
Once the Single European Act enters into force the Commission shall submit a comprehensive proposal to the Council, the purpose of which will be to make such amendments to the structure and operational rules of the existing structural Funds (European Agricultural Guidance and Guarantee Fund, Guidance Section, European Social Fund, European Regional Development Fund) as are necessary to clarify and rationalise their tasks in order to contribute to the achievement of the objectives set out in Article 130a and Article 130c, to increase their efficiency and to co-ordinate their activities between themselves and with the operations of the existing financial instruments. The Council shall act unanimously on this proposal within a period of one year, after consulting the European Parliament and the Economic and Social Committee.

Article 130e
After adoption of the decision referred to in Article 130d, implementing decisions relating to the European Regional Development Fund shall be taken by the Council, acting by a qualified majority on a proposal from the Commission and in cooperation with the European Parliament.

With regard to the European Agricultural Guidance and Guarantee Fund, Guidance Section and the European Social Fund, Articles 43, 126 and 127 remain applicable respectively.

TITLE VI
RESEARCH AND TECHNOLOGICAL DEVELOPMENT[1]

1 Title VI and Articles therein added by the Single European Act, art 24.

Article 130f
1. The Community's aim shall be to strengthen the scientific and technological basis of European industry and to encourage it to become more competitive at international level.

2. In order to achieve this, it shall encourage undertakings including small and medium-sized undertakings, research centres and universities in their research and technological development activities; it shall support their efforts to co-operate with one another, aiming, notably, at enabling undertakings to exploit the Community's internal market potential to the full, in particular through the opening up of national public contracts, the definition of common standards and the removal of legal and fiscal barriers to that cooperation.

3. In the achievement of these aims, special account shall be taken of the connection between the common research and technological development effort, the establishment of the internal market and the implementation of common policies, particularly as regards competition and trade.

Article 130g
In pursuing these objectives the Community shall carry out the following activities, complementing the activities carried out in the Member States:

(a)   implementation of research, technological development and demonstration programmes, by promoting co-operation with undertakings, research centres and universities;

(b)   promotion of co-operation in the field of Community research, technological development and demonstration with third countries and international organisations;

(c)	dissemination and optimisation of the results of activities in Community research, technological development and demonstration;
(d)	stimulation of the training and mobility of researchers in the Community.

Article 130h
Member States shall, in liaison with the Commission, co-ordinate among themselves the policies and programmes carried out at national level. In close contact with the Member States, the Commission may take any useful initiative to promote such co-ordination.

Article 130i
1. The Community shall adopt a multi-annual framework programme setting out all its activities. The framework programme shall lay down the scientific and technical objectives, define their respective priorities, set out the main lines of the activities envisaged and fix the amount deemed necessary, the detailed rules for financial participation by the Community in the programme as a whole and the breakdown of this amount between the various activities envisaged.

2. The framework programme may be adapted or supplemented, as the situation changes.

Article 130k
The framework programme shall be implemented through specific programmes developed within each activity. Each specific programme shall define the detailed rules for implementing it, fix its duration and provide for the means deemed necessary.

The Council shall define the detailed arrangements for the dissemination of knowledge resulting from the specific programmes.

Article 130l
In implementing the multi-annual framework programme, supplementary programmes may be decided on involving the participation of certain Member States only, which shall finance them subject to possible Community participation.

The Council shall adopt the rules applicable to supplementary programmes, particularly as regards the dissemination of knowledge and the access of other Member States.

Article 130m
In implementing the multi-annual framework programme, the Community may make provision, with the agreement of the Member States concerned, for participation in research and development programmes undertaken by several Member States, including participation in the structures created for the execution of those programmes.

Article 130n
In implementing the multi-annual framework programme, the Community may make provision for co-operation in Community research, technological development and demonstration with third countries or international organisations.

The detailed arrangements for such co-operation may be the subject of international agreements between the Community and the third parties concernedwhich shall be negotiated and concluded in accordance with Article 228.

Article 130o

The Community may set up joint undertakings or any other structure necessary for the efficient execution of programmes of Community research, technological development and demonstration.

Article 130p

1. The detailed arrangements for financing each programme, including any Community contribution, shall be established at the time of the adoption of the programme.

2. The amount of the Community's annual contribution shall be laid down under the budgetary procedure, without prejudice to other possible methods of Community financing. The estimated cost of the specific programmes must not in aggregate exceed the financial provision in the framework programme.

Article 130q

1. The Council shall, acting unanimously on a proposal from the Commission and after consulting the European Parliament and the Economic and Social Committee, adopt the provisions referred to in Articles 130i and 130o.

2. The Council shall, acting by a qualified majority on a proposal from the Commission, after consulting the Economic and Social Committee, and in co-operation with the European Parliament, adopt the provisions referred to in Articles 130k, 130l, 130m, 130n and 130p. The adoption of these supplementary programmes shall also require the agreement of the Member States concerned.

TITLE VII
ENVIRONMENT[1]

1 Title VII and Articles therein added by the Single European Act, art 25.

Article 130r

1. Action by the Community relating to the environment shall have the following objectives:
  (i) to preserve, protect and improve the quality of the environment;
  (ii) to contribute towards protecting human health;
  (iii) to ensure a prudent and rational utilisation of natural resources.
2. Action by the Community relating to the environment shall be based on the principles that preventive action should be taken, that environmental damage should as a priority be rectified at source, and that the polluter should pay. Environmental protection requirements shall be a component of the Community's other policies.

3. In preparing its action relating to the environment, the Community shall take account of:
  (i) available scientific and technical data;
  (ii) environmental conditions in the various regions of the Community;
  (iii) the potential benefits and costs of action or of lack of action;
  (iv) the economic and social development of the Community as a whole and the balanced development of its regions.

4. The Community shall take action relating to the environment to the extent to which the objectives referred to in paragraph 1 can be attained better at Community level than at the level of the individual Member States. Without prejudice to certain measures of a Community nature, the Member States shall finance and implement the other measures.

5. Within their respective spheres of competence, the Community and the

Member States shall co-operate with third countries and with the relevant international organisations. The arrangements for Community co-operation may be the subject of agreements between the Community and the third parties concerned, which shall be negotiated and concluded in accordance with Article 228.

The previous paragraph shall be without prejudice to Member States' competence to negotiate in international bodies and to conclude international agreements.

Article 130s
The Council, acting unanimously on a proposal from the Commission and after consulting the European Parliament and the Economic and Social Committee, shall decide what action is to be taken by the Community.

The Council shall, under the conditions laid down in the preceding sub-paragraph, define those matters on which decisions are to be taken by a qualified majority.

Article 130t
The protective measures adopted in common pursuant to Article 130s shall not prevent any Member State from maintaining or introducing more stringent protective measures compatible with this Treaty.

PART FOUR

ASSOCIATION OF THE OVERSEAS COUNTRIES AND TERRITORIES

Article 131
The Member States agree to associate with the Community the non-European countries and territories which have special relations with Belgium, Denmark, France, Italy, the Netherlands and the United Kingdom[1]. These countries and territories (hereinafter called the "countries and territories") are listed in Annex IV to this Treaty.

The purpose of association shall be to promote the economic and social development of the countries and territories and to establish close economic relations between them and the Community as a whole.

In accordance with the principles set out in the Preamble to this Treaty, association shall serve primarily to further the interests and prosperity of the inhabitants of these countries and territories in order to lead them to the economic, social and cultural development to which they aspire.

1 As amended by the First Act of Accession."Denmark" added by the Greenland Treaty, art 2.

Article 132
Association shall have the following objectives :

1. Member States shall apply to their trade with the countries and territories the same treatment as they accord each other pursuant to this Treaty.

2. Each country or territory shall apply to its trade with Member States and with the other countries and territories the same treatment as that which it applies to the European State with which it has special relations.

3. The Member States shall contribute to the investments required for the progressive development of these countries and territories.

4. For investments financed by the Community, participation in tenders and supplies shall be open on equal terms to all natural and legal persons who are nationals of a Member State or of one of the countries and territories.

5. In relations between Member States and the countries and territories the right of establishment of nationals and companies or firms shall be regulated in accordance with the provisions and procedures laid down in the Chapter relating to the right of establishment and on a non-discriminatory basis, subject to any special provisions laid down pursuant to Article 136.

Article 133

1. Customs duties on imports into the Member States of goods originating in the countries and territories shall be completely abolished in conformity with the progressive abolition of customs duties between Member States in accordance with the provisions of this Treaty.

2. Customs duties on imports into each country or territory from Member States or from the other countries or territories shall be progressively abolished in accordance with the provisions of Articles 12, 13, 14, 15 and 17.

3. The countries and territories may, however, levy customs duties which meet the needs of their development and industrialisation or produce revenue for their budgets.

The duties referred to in the preceding sub-paragraph shall nevertheless be progressively reduced to the level of those imposed on imports of products from the Member State with which each country or territory has special relations. The percentages and the timetable of the reductions provided for under this Treaty shall apply to the difference between the duty imposed on a product coming from the Member State which has special relations with the country or territory concerned and the duty imposed on the same product coming from within the Community on entry into the importing country or territory.

4. Paragraph 2 shall not apply to countries and territories which, by reason of the particular international obligations by which they are bound, already apply a non-discriminatory customs tariff when this Treaty enters into force.

5. The introduction of or any change in customs duties imposed on goods imported into the countries and territories shall not, either in law or in fact, give rise to any direct or indirect discrimination between imports from the various Member States.

Article 134

If the level of the duties applicable to goods from a third country on entry into a country or territory is liable, when the provisions of Article 133 (1) have been applied, to cause deflections of trade to the detriment of any Member State, the latter may request the Commission to propose to the other Member States the measures needed to remedy the situation.

Article 135

Subject to the provisions relating to public health, public security or public policy, freedom of movement within Member States for workers from the countries and territories, and within the countries and territories for workers from Member States, shall be governed by agreements to be concluded subsequently with the unanimous approval of Member States.

Article 136

For an initial period of five years after the entry into force of this Treaty, the details of and procedure for the association of the countries and territories with the Community shall be determined by an Implementing Convention annexed to this Treaty.

Before the Convention referred to in the preceding paragraph expires, the Council shall, acting unanimously, lay down provisions for a further period, on the basis of the experience acquired and of the principles set out in this Treaty.

Article 136a[1]

The provisions of Articles 131 to 136 shall apply to Greenland, subject to the specific provisions for Greenland set out in the Protocol on special arrangements for Greenland, annexed to this Treaty.

1 As added by the Greenland Treaty, art 3 (1).

PART FIVE

INSTITUTIONS OF THE COMMUNITY

TITLE 1
PROVISIONS GOVERNING THE INSTITUTIONS

CHAPTER 1-THE INSTITUTIONS

Section 1-The European Parliament

Article 137

The European Parliament, which shall consist of representatives of the peoples of the States brought together in the Community, shall exercise the advisory and supervisory powers which are conferred upon it by this Treaty.

Article 138 [1]

1 Paragraphs 1 and 2 lapsed on 17 July 1979 ~~in accordance with~~ the Act concerning the election of the representatives of the European Parliament.

See Act concerning the election of the representatives of the European Parliament, art 1:

The representatives in the European Parliament of the peoples of the States brought together in the Community shall be elected by direct universal suffrage.

See Act concerning the election of the representatives of the European Parliament, art 2 :

The number of representatives elected in each Member State is as follows :

Belgium	24
Denmark	16
Germany	81
Greece	24
Spain	60
France	81
Ireland	15
Italy	81
Luxembourg	6
Netherlands	25
Portugal	24
United Kingdom	81

3. The European Parliament shall draw up proposals for elections by direct universal suffrage in accordance with a uniform procedure in all Member States.[1]

The Council shall, acting unanimously, lay down the appropriate provisions which it shall recommend to Member States for adoption in accordance with their respective constitutional requirements.

1 See also the Act concerning the election of the representatives of the European Parliament, art 7(1), (2).

Article 139

The European Parliament shall hold an annual session. It shall meet, without requiring to be convened, on the second Tuesday in March.[1]

The European Parliament may meet in extraordinary session at the request of a majority of its members or at the request of the Council or of the Commission.

1 As amended by the Merger Treaty, art 27 (1).

Article 140

The European Parliament shall elect its President and its officers from among its members.

Members of the Commission may attend all meetings and shall, at their request, be heard on behalf of the Commission.

The Commission shall reply orally or in writing to questions put to it by the European Parliament or by its members.

The Council shall be heard by the European Parliament in accordance with the conditions laid down by the Council in its rules of procedure.

Article 141

Save as otherwise provided in this Treaty, the European Parliament shall act by an absolute majority of the votes cast.

The rules of procedure shall determine the quorum.

Article 142

The European Parliament shall adopt its rules of procedure, acting by a majority of its members.

The proceedings of the European Parliament shall be published in the manner laid down in its rules of procedure.

Article 143

The European Parliament shall discuss in open session the annual general report submitted to it by the Commission.

Article 144

If a motion of censure on the activities of the Commission is tabled before it, the European Parliament shall not vote thereon until at least three days after the motion has been tabled and only by open vote.

If the motion of censure is carried by a two-thirds majority of the votes cast, representing a majority of the members of the European Parliament, the members of the Commission shall resign as a body. They shall continue to deal with current business until they are replaced in accordance with Article 158.

Section 2-The Council

Article 145

To ensure that the objectives set out in this Treaty are attained, the Council shall, in accordance with the provisions of this Treaty:
- ensure co-ordination of the general economic policies of the Member States;
- have power to take decisions.

177

- confer on the Commission, in the acts which the Council adopts, powers for the implementation of the rules which the Council lays down. The Council may impose certain requirements in respect of the exercise of these powers. The Council may also reserve the right, in specific cases, to exercise directly implementing powers itself. The procedures referred to above must be consonant with principles and

rules to be laid down in advance by the Council, acting unanimously on a proposal from the Commission and after obtaining the opinion of the European Parliament.[1]

1 As amended by the Single European Act, art 10.

Article 146 [1]

1 Repealed by the Merger Treaty, art 7.

Article 147 [1]

1 Repealed by the Merger Treaty, art 7.

Article 148

1. Save as otherwise provided in this Treaty, the Council shall act by a majority of its members.

[2. Where the Council is required to act by a qualified majority, the votes of its members shall be weighted as follows:

Belgium	5
Denmark	3
Germany	10
Greece	5
Spain	8
France	10
Ireland	3
Italy	10
Luxembourg	2
Netherlands	5
Portugal	5
United Kingdom	10

For their adoption, acts of the Council shall require at least:

- 54 votes in favour where this Treaty requires them to be adopted on a proposal from the Commission,
- 54 votes in favour, cast by at least eight members, in other cases.[1]

3. Abstentions by members present in person or represented shall not prevent the adoption by the Council of acts which require unanimity.

1 As amended by the Third Act of Accession, art 14.

Article 149 [1]

1. Where, in pursuance of this Treaty, the Council acts on a proposal from the Commission, unanimity shall be required for an act constituting an amendment to that proposal.

2. Where, in pursuance of this Treaty, the Council acts in co-operation with the European Parliament, the following procedure shall apply:
(a)The Council, acting by a qualified majority under the conditions of paragraph 1, on a proposal from the Commission and after obtaining the opinion of the European Parliament, shall adopt a common position.

(b)The Council's common position shall be communicated to the European Parliament. The Council and the Commission shall inform the European Parliament fully of the reasons which led the Council to adopt its common position and also of the Commission's position. If, within three months of such communication, the European Parliament approves this common position or has not taken a decision within that period, the Council shall definitively adopt the act in question in accordance with the common position.

(c)The European Parliament may within the period of three months referred to in point (b), by an absolute majority of its component members, propose amendments to the Council's common position. The European Parliament may also, by the same majority, reject the Council's common position. The result of the proceedings shall be transmitted to the Council and the Commission.

If the European Parliament has rejected the Council's common position, unanimity shall be required for the Council to act on a second reading.

(d)The Commission shall, within a period of one month, re-examine the proposal on the basis of which the Council adopted its common position, by taking into account the amendments proposed by the European Parliament.

The Commission shall forward to the Council, at the same time as its re-examined proposal, the amendments of the European Parliament which it has not accepted, and shall express its opinion on them. The Council may adopt these amendments unanimously.

e)The Council, acting by a qualified majority, shall adopt the proposal as re-examined by the Commission.

Unanimity shall be required for the Council to amend the proposal as re-examined by the Commission.

(f)In the cases referred to in points (c), (d) and (e), the Council shall be required to act within a period of three months. If no decision is taken within this period, the Commission proposal shall be deemed not have been adopted.

(g)The periods referred to in points (b) and (f) may be extended by a maximum of one month by common accord between the Council and the European Parliament.

3. As long as the Council has not acted, the Commission may alter its proposal at any time during the procedures mentioned in paragraphs 1 and 2.

1 As replaced by the Single European Act, art 7.

Article 150
Where a vote is taken, any member of the Council may also act on behalf of not more than one other member.

Article 151 [1]

1 Repealed by the Merger Treaty, art 7.

Article 152
The Council may request the Commission to undertake any studies which the Council considers desirable for the attainment of the common objectives, and to submit to it any appropriate proposals.

Article 153
The Council shall, after receiving an opinion from the Commission, determine the rules governing the committees provided for in this Treaty.

Article 154 [1]

1 Repealed by the Merger Treaty, art 7.

Section 3-The Commission

Article 155

In order to ensure the proper functioning and development of the common market, the Commission shall:

- ensure that the provisions of this Treaty and the measures taken by the institutions pursuant thereto are applied;
- formulate recommendations or deliver opinions on matters dealt with in this Treaty, if it expressly so provides or if the Commission considers it necessary;
- have its own power of decision and participate in the shaping of measures taken by the Council and by the European Parliament in the manner provided for in this Treaty;
- exercise the powers conferred on it by the Council for the implementation of the rules laid down by the latter.

Articles 156 to 163 [1]

1 Repealed by the Merger Treaty, art 19.

Section 4 -The Court of Justice

Article 164

The Court of Justice shall ensure that in the interpretation and application of this Treaty the law is observed.

Article 165

The Court of Justice shall consist of 13 Judges.[1]

The Court of Justice shall sit in plenary session. It may, however, form Chambers, each consisting of three or five Judges, either to undertake certain preparatory inquiries or to adjudicate on particular categories of cases in accordance with rules laid down for these purposes.

Whenever the Court of Justice hears cases brought before it by a Member State or by one of the institutions of the Community or, to the extent that the Chambers of the Court do not have the requisite jurisdiction under the Rules of Procedure, has to give preliminary rulings on questions submitted to it pursuant to Article 177, it shall sit in plenary session.[2]

Should the Court of Justice so request, the Council may, acting unanimously, increase the number of Judges and make the necessary adjustments to the second and third paragraphs of this Article and to the second paragraph of Article 167.

1 As amended by the Third Act of Accession.
2 As amended by Council Decision (EEC, Euratom, ECSC) 74/584.

Article 166

[The Court of Justice shall be assisted by six Advocates-General.[1]

It shall be the duty of the Advocate-General, acting with complete impartiality and independence, to make, in open court, reasoned submissions on cases brought before the Court of Justice, in order to assist the Court in the performance of the task assigned to it in Article 164.

Should the Court of Justice so request, the Council may, acting unanimously, increase the number of Advocates-General and make the necessary adjustments to the third paragraph of Article 167.

1 Amended by the Third Act of Accession.

Article 167 [1]

The Judges and Advocates-General shall be chosen from persons whose independence is beyond doubt and who possess the qualifications required for appointment to the highest judicial offices in their respective countries or who are jurisconsults of recognised competence; they shall be appointed by common accord of the Governments of the Member States for a term of six years.

Every three years there shall be a partial replacement of the Judges. Seven and six Judges shall be replaced alternately.

Every three years there shall be a partial replacement of the Advocates General. Three Advocates-General shall be replaced on each occassion.

Retiring Judges and Advocates-General shall be eligible for reappointment.

The Judges shall elect the President of the Court of Justice from among their number for a term of three years. He may be re-elected.

1 As amended by the Third Act of Accession.

Article 168

The Court of Justice shall appoint its Registrar and lay down the rules governing his service.

Article 168a [1]

1. At the request of the Court of Justice and after consulting the Commission and the European Parliament, the Council may, acting unanimously, attach to the Court of Justice a court with jurisdiction to hear and determine at first instance, subject to a right of appeal to the Court of Justice on points of law only and in accordance with the conditions laid down by the Statute, certain classes of action or proceeding brought by natural or legal persons. That court shall not be competent to hear and determine actions brought by Member States or by Community institutions or questions referred for a preliminary ruling under Article 177.

2. The Council, following the procedure laid down in paragraph 1, shall determine the composition of that court and adopt the necessary adjustments and additional provisions to the Statute of the Court of Justice. Unless the Council decides otherwise, the provisions of this Treaty relating to the Court of Justice, in particular the provisions of the Protocol on the Statute of the Court of Justice, shall apply to that court.

3. The members of that court shall be chosen from persons whose independence is beyond doubt and who possess the ability required for appointment to judicial office; they shall be appointed by common accord of the Governments of the Member States for a term of six years. The membership shall be partially renewed every three years. Retiring members shall be eligible for re-appointment.

4. That court shall establish its rules of procedure in agreement with the Court of Justice. Those rules shall require the unanimous approval of the Council.

1 Added by the Single European Act, art 11.

Article 169

If the Commission considers that a Member State has failed to fulfil an obligation under this Treaty, it shall deliver a reasoned opinion on the matter after giving the State concerned the opportunity to submit its observations.

If the State concerned does not comply with the opinion within the period laid down by the Commission, the latter may bring the matter before the Court of Justice.

Article 170

A Member State which considers that another Member State has failed to fulfil an obligation under this Treaty may bring the matter before the Court of Justice.

Before a Member State brings an action against another Member State for an alleged infringement of an obligation under this Treaty, it shall bring the matter before the Commission.

The Commission shall deliver a reasoned opinion after each of the States concerned has been given the opportunity to submit its own case and its observations on the other party's case both orally and in writing.

If the Commission has not delivered an opinion within three months of the date on which the matter was brought before it, the absence of such opinion shall not prevent the matter from being brought before the Court of Justice.

Article 171

If the Court of Justice finds that a Member State has failed to fulfil an obligation under this Treaty, the State shall be required to take the necessary measures to comply with the judgment of the Court of Justice.

Article 172

Regulations made by the Council pursuant to the provisions of this Treaty may give the Court of Justice unlimited jurisdiction in regard to the penalties provided for in such regulations.

Article 173

The Court of Justice shall review the legality of acts of the Council and the Commission other than recommendations or opinions. It shall for this purpose have jurisdiction in actions brought by a Member State, the Council or the Commission on grounds of lack of competence, infringement of an essential procedural requirement, infringement of this Treaty or of any rule of law relating to its application, or misuse of powers.

Any natural or legal person may, under the same conditions, institute proceedings against a decision addressed to that person or against a decision which, although in the form of a regulation or a decision addressed to another person, is of direct and individual concern to the former.

The proceedings provided for in this Article shall be instituted within two months of the publication of the measure, or of its notification to the plaintiff, or, in the absence thereof, of the day on which it came to the knowledge of the latter, as the case may be.

Article 174

If the action is well founded, the Court of Justice shall declare the act concerned to be void.

In the case of a regulation, however, the Court of Justice shall, if it considers this necessary, state which of the effects of the regulation which it has declared void shall be considered as definitive.

Article 175

Should the Council or the Commission, in infringement of this Treaty, fail to act, the Member States and the other institutions of the Community may bring an action before the Court of Justice to have the infringement established.

The action shall be admissible only if the institution concerned has first been called upon to act. If, within two months of being so called upon, the nstitution concerned has not defined its position, the action may be brought within a further period of two months.

Any natural or legal person may, under the conditions laid down in the preceding paragraphs, complain to the Court of Justice that an institution of the Community has failed to address to that person any act other than a recommendation or an opinion.

Article 176
The institution whose act has been declared void or whose failure to act has been declared contrary to this Treaty shall be required to take the necessary measures to comply with the judgment of the Court of Justice.

This obligation shall not affect any obligation which may result from the application of the second paragraph of Article 215.

Article 177
The Court of Justice shall have jurisdiction to give preliminary rulings concerning:
- (a) the interpretation of this Treaty;
- (b) the validity and interpretation of acts of the institutions of the Community;
- (c) the interpretation of the statutes of bodies established by an act of the Council, where those statutes so provide.

Where such a question is raised before any court or tribunal of a Member State, that court or tribunal may, if it considers that a decision on the question is necessary to enable it to give judgment, request the Court of Justice to give a ruling thereon.

Where any such question is raised in a case pending before a court or tribunal of a Member State, against whose decisions there is no judicial remedy under national law, that court or tribunal shall bring the matter before the Court of Justice.

Article 178
The Court of Justice shall have jurisdiction in disputes relating to the compensation for damage provided for in the second paragraph of Article 215.

Article 179
The Court of Justice shall have jurisdiction in any dispute between the Community and its servants within the limits and under the conditions laid down in the Staff Regulations or the Conditions of Employment.

Article 180
The Court of Justice shall, within the limits hereinafter laid down, have jurisdiction in disputes concerning:
- (a) the fulfilment by Member States of obligations under the Statute of the European Investment Bank. In this connection, the Board of Directors of the Bank shall enjoy the powers conferred upon the Commission by Article 169;
- (b) measures adopted by the Board of Governors of the Bank. In this connection, any Member State, the Commission or the Board of Directors of the Bank may institute proceedings under the conditions laid down in Article 173;
- (c) measures adopted by the Board of Directors of the Bank. Proceedings against such measures may be instituted only by Member States or by the Commission, under the conditions laid down in Article 173, and solely on the grounds of non-compliance with the procedure provided for in Article 21 (2), (5), (6) and (7) of the Statute of the Bank.

Article 181

The Court of Justice shall have jurisdiction to give judgment pursuant to any arbitration clause contained in a contract concluded by or on behalf of the Community, whether that contract be governed by public or private law.

Article 182

The Court of Justice shall have jurisdiction in any dispute between Member States which relates to the subject matter of this Treaty if the dispute is submitted to it under a special agreement between the parties.

Article 183

Save where jurisdiction is conferred on the Court of Justice by this Treaty, disputes to which the Community is a party shall not on that ground be excluded from the jurisdiction of the courts or tribunals of the Member States.

Article 184

Notwithstanding the expiry of the period laid down in the third paragraph of Article 173, any party may, in proceedings in which a regulation of the Council or of the Commission is in issue, plead the grounds specified in the first paragraph of Article 173, in order to invoke before the Court of Justice the inapplicability of that regulation.

Article 185

Actions brought before the Court of Justice shall not have suspensory effect. The Court of Justice may, however, if it considers that circumstances so require, order that application of the contested act be suspended.

Article 186

The Court of Justice may in any cases before it prescribe any necessary interim measures.

Article 187

The judgments of the Court of Justice shall be enforceable under the conditions laid down in Article 192.

Article 188

The Statute of the Court of Justice is laid down in a separate Protocol.

The Council may, acting unanimously at the request of the Court of Justice and after consulting the Commission and the European Parliament, amend the provisions of Title III of the Statute.[1]

The Court of Justice shall adopt its rules of procedure. These shall require the unanimous approval of the Council.

1 As amended by the Single European Act, art 12.

CHAPTER 2-PROVISIONS COMMON TO SEVERAL INSTITUTIONS

Article 189

In order to carry out their task the Council and the Commission shall, in accordance with the provisions of this Treaty, make regulations, issue directives, take decisions, make recommendations or deliver opinions.

A regulation shall have general application. It shall be binding in its entirety and directly applicable in all Member States.

A directive shall be binding, as to the result to be achieved, upon each Member State to which it is addressed, but shall leave to the national authorities the choice of form and methods.

A decision shall be binding in its entirety upon those to whom it is addressed. Recommendations and opinions shall have no binding force.

Article 190
Regulations, directives and decisions of the Council and of the Commission shall state the reasons on which they are based and shall refer to any proposals or opinions which were required to be obtained pursuant to this Treaty.

Article 191
Regulations shall be published in the Official Journal of the Community. They shall enter into force on the date specified in them or, in the absence thereof, on the twentieth day following their publication.

Directives and decisions shall be notified to those to whom they are addressed and shall take effect upon such notification.

Article 192
Decisions of the Council or of the Commission which impose a pecuniary obligation on persons other than States shall be enforceable.

Enforcement shall be governed by the rules of civil procedure in force in the State in the territory of which it is carried out. The order for its enforcement shall be appended to the decision, without other formality than verification of the authenticity of the decision, by the national authority which the Government of each Member State shall designate for this purpose and shall make known to the Commission and to the Court of Justice.

When these formalities have been completed on application by the party concerned, the latter may proceed to enforcement in accordance with the national law, by bringing the matter directly before the competent authority.

Enforcement may be suspended only by a decision of the Court of Justice. However, the courts of the country concerned shall have jurisdiction over complaints that enforcement is being carried out in an irregular manner.

CHAPTER 3-THE ECONOMIC AND SOCIAL COMMITTEE

Article 193
An Economic and Social Committee is hereby established. It shall have advisory status.

The Committee shall consist of representatives of the various categories of economic and social activity, in particular, representatives of producers, farmers, carriers, workers, dealers, craftsmen, professional occupations and representatives of the general public.

Article 194
The number of members of the Committee shall be as follows:

Belgium	12
Denmark	9
Germany	24
Greece	12
Spain	21
France	24
Ireland	9
Italy	24
Luxembourg	6
Netherlands	12
Portugal	12
United Kingdom	24¹

The members of the Committee shall be appointed by the Council, acting unanimously, for four years. Their appointments shall be renewable.

The members of the Committee shall be appointed in their personal capacity and may not be bound by any mandatory instructions.

1 As amended by the Third Act of Accession.

Article 195
1. For the appointment of the members of the Committee, each Member State shall provide the Council with a list containing twice as many candidates as there are seats allotted to its nationals.

The composition of the Committee shall take account of the need to ensure adequate representation of the various categories of economic and social activity.

2. The Council shall consult the Commission. It may obtain the opinion of European bodies which are representative of the various economic and social sectors to which the activities of the Community are of concern.

Article 196
The Committee shall elect its chairman and officers from among its members for a term of two years.

It shall adopt its rules of procedure and shall submit them to the Council for its approval, which must be unanimous.

The Committee shall be convened by its chairman at the request of the Council or of the Commission.

Article 197
The Committee shall include specialised sections for the principal fields covered by this Treaty.

In particular, it shall contain an agricultural section and a transport section, which are the subject of special provisions in the Titles relating to agriculture and transport.

These specialised sections shall operate within the general terms of reference of the Committee. They may not be consulted independently of the Committee.

Sub-committees may also be established within the Committee to prepare, on specific questions or in specific fields, draft opinions to be submitted to the Committee for its consideration.

The rules of procedure shall lay down the methods of composition and the terms of reference of the specialised sections and of the sub-committees.

Article 198
The Committee must be consulted by the Council or by the Commission where this Treaty so provides. The Committee may be consulted by these institutions in all cases in which they consider it appropriate.

The Council or the Commission shall, if it considers it necessary, set the Committee, for the submission of its opinion, a time limit which may not be less than ten days from the date on which the chairman receives notification to this effect. Upon expiry of the time limit, the absence of an opinion shall not prevent further action.

The opinion of the Committee and that of the specialised section, together with a record of the proceedings, shall be forwarded to the Council and to the Commission.

TITLE II
FINANCIAL PROVISIONS

Article 199
All items of revenue and expenditure of the Community, including those relating to the European Social Fund, shall be included in estimates to be drawn up for each financial year and shall be shown in the budget.

The revenue and expenditure shown in the budget shall be in balance.

Article 200
1. The budget revenue shall include, irrespective of any other revenue, financial contributions of Member States on the following scale:

Belgium	7.9
Germany	28
France	28
Italy	28
Luxembourg	0.2
Netherlands	7.9

2. The financial contributions of Member States to cover the expenditure of the European Social Fund, however, shall be determined on the following scale:

Belgium	8.8
Germany	32
France	32
Italy	20
Luxembourg	0.2
Netherlands	7

3. The scales may be modified by the Council, acting unanimously.

Article 201
The Commission shall examine the conditions under which the financial contributions Member States provided for in Article 200 could be replaced by the Community's own resources, in particular by revenue accruing from the common customs tariff when it has been finally introduced.

To this end, the Commission shall submit proposals to the Council.

After consulting the European Parliament on these proposals the Council may, acting unanimously, lay down the appropriate provisions, which it shall recommend to the Member States for adoption in accordance with their respective constitutional requirements.

Article 202
The expenditure shown in the budget shall be authorised for one financial year, unless the regulations made pursuant to Article 209 provide otherwise.

In accordance with conditions to be laid down pursuant to Article 209, any appropriations, other than those relating to staff expenditure, that are unexpended at the end of the financial year may be carried forward to the next financial year only.

Appropriations shall be classified under different chapters grouping items of expenditure according to their nature or purpose and subdivided, as far as may be necessary, in accordance with the regulations made pursuant to Article 209.

The expenditure of the European Parliament, the Council, the Commission and the Court of Justice shall be set out in separate parts of the budget, without prejudice to special arrangements for certain common items of expenditure.

Article 203 [1]
1. The financial year shall run from 1 January to 31 December.

2. Each institution of the Community shall, before 1 July, draw up estimates of its expenditure. The Commission shall consolidate these estimates in a preliminary draft budget. It shall attach thereto an opinion which may contain different estimates.

The preliminary draft budget shall contain an estimate of revenue and an estimate of expenditure.

3. The Commission shall place the preliminary draft budget before the Council not later than 1 September of the year preceding that in which the budget is to be implemented.

The Council shall consult the Commission and, where appropriate, the other institutions concerned whenever it intends to depart from the preliminary draft budget.

The Council, acting by a qualified majority, shall establish the draft budget and forward it to the European Parliament.

4. The draft budget shall be placed before the European Parliament not later than 5 October of the year preceding that in which the budget is to be implemented.

The European Parliament shall have the right to amend the draft budget, acting by a majority of its members, and to propose to the Council, acting by an absolute majority of the votes cast, modifications to the draft budget relating to expenditure necessarily resulting from this Treaty or from acts adopted in accordance therewith.

If, within 45 days of the draft budget being placed before it, the European Parliament has given its approval, the budget shall stand as finally adopted. If within this period the European Parliament has not amended the draft budget nor proposed any modifications thereto, the budget shall be deemed to be finally adopted.

If within this period the European Parliament has adopted amendments or proposed modifications, the draft budget together with the amendments or proposed modifications shall be forwarded to the Council.

5. After discussing the draft budget with the Commission and, where appropriate, with the other institutions concerned, the Council shall act under the following conditions:
    (a)   the Council may, acting by a qualified majority, modify any of the amendments adopted by the European Parliament;
    (b)   with regard to the proposed modifications:
- where a modification proposed by the European Parliament does not have the effect of increasing the total amount of the expenditure of an institution, owing in particular to the fact that the increase in expenditure which it would involve would be expressly compensated by one or more proposed modifications

correspondingly reducing expenditure, the Council may, acting by a qualified majority, reject the proposed modification. In the absence of a decision to reject it, the proposed modification shall stand as accepted;
- where a modification proposed by the European Parliament has the effect of increasing the total amount of the expenditure of an institution, the Council may, acting by a qualified majority, accept this proposed modification. In the absence of a decision to accept it, the proposed modification shall stand as rejected;
- where, in pursuance of one of the two preceding sub-paragraphs, the Council has rejected a proposed modification, it may, acting by a qualified majority, either retain the amount shown in the draft budget or fix another amount.

The draft budget shall be modified on the basis of the proposed modifications accepted by the Council.

If, within 15 days of the draft budget being placed before it, the Council has not modified any of the amendments adopted by the European Parliament and if the modifications proposed by the latter have been accepted, the budget shall be deemed to be finally adopted. The Council shall inform the European Parliament that it has not modified any of the amendments and that the proposed modifications have been accepted.

If within this period the Council has modified one or more of the amendments adopted by the European Parliament or if the modifications proposed by the latter have been rejected or modified, the modified draft budget shall again be forwarded to the European Parliament. The Council shall inform the European Parliament of the results of its deliberations.

6. Within 15 days of the draft budget being placed before it, the European Parliament, which shall have been notified of the action taken on its proposed modifications, may, acting by a majority of its members and three-fifths of the votes cast, amend or reject the modifications to its amendments made by the Council and shall adopt the budget accordingly. If within this period the European Parliament has not acted, the budget shall be deemed to be finally adopted.

7. When the procedure provided for in this Article has been completed, the President of the European Parliament shall declare that the budget has been finally adopted.

8. However, the European Parliament acting by a majority of its members and two-thirds of the votes cast, may if there are important reasons reject the draft budget and ask for a new draft to be submitted to it.

9. A maximum rate of increase in relation to the expenditure of the same type to be incurred during the current year shall be fixed annually for the total expenditure other than that necessarily resulting from this Treaty or from acts adopted in accordance therewith.

The Commission shall, after consulting the Economic Policy Committee, declare what this maximum rate is as it results from:
- the trend, in terms of volume, of the gross national product within the Community;
- the average variation in the budgets of the Member States;
and
- the trend of the cost of living during the preceding financial year.

The maximum rate shall be communicated, before 1 May, to all the institutions of the Community. The latter shall be required to conform to this during the budgetary procedure, subject to the provisions of the fourth and fifth sub-paragraphs of this paragraph.

If, in respect of expenditure other than that necessarily resulting from this Treaty or from acts adopted in accordance therewith, the actual rate of increase in the draft budget, established by the Council is over half the maximum rate, the European Parliament may, exercising its right of amendment, further increase the total amount of that expenditure to a limit not exceeding half the maximum rate.

Where the European Parliament, the Council or the Commission consider that the activities of the Communities require that the rate determined according to the procedure laid down in this paragraph should be exceeded, another rate may be fixed by agreement between the Council, acting by a qualified majority, and the European Parliament, acting by a majority of its members and three-fifths of the votes cast.

10. Each institution shall exercise the powers conferred upon it by this Article, with due regard for the provisions of the Treaty and for acts adopted in accordance therewith, in particular those relating to the Communities' own resources and to the balance between revenue and expenditure.

1 As substituted by the Financial Provisions Treaty, art 12

Article 204 [1]

If, at the beginning of a financial year, the budget has not yet been voted, a sum equivalent to not more than one-twelfth of the budget appropriations for the preceding financial year may be spent each month in respect of any chapter or other subdivision of the budget in accordance with the provisions of the Regulations made pursuant to Article 209; this arrangement shall not, how-ever, have the effect of placing at the disposal of the Commission appropriations in excess of one-twelfth of those provided for in the draft budget in course of preparation.

The Council may, acting by a qualified majority, provided that the other conditions laid down in the first sub-paragraph are observed, authorise expenditure in excess of one-twelfth.

If the decision relates to expenditure which does not necessarily result from this Treaty or from acts adopted in accordance therewith, the Council shall forward it immediately to the European Parliament within 30 days the European Parliament, acting by a majority of its members and three-fifths of the votes case, may adopt a different decision on the expenditure in excess of the one-twelfth referred to in the first sub-paragraph. This part of the decision of the Council shall be suspended until the European Parliament has taken its decision. If within the period the European Parliament has not taken a decision which differs from the decision of the Council, the latter shall be deemed to be finally adopted.

The decisions referred to in the second and third sub-paragraphs shall lay down the necessary measures relating to resources to ensure application of this Article.

1 As substituted by the Financial Provisions Treaty, art 13.

Article 205

The Commission shall implement the budget, in accordance with the provisions of the regulations made pursuant to Article 209, on its own responsibility and within the limits of the appropriations.

The regulations shall lay down detailed rules for each institution concerning its part in effecting its own expenditure.

Within the budget, the Commission may, subject to the limits and conditions laid down in the regulations made pursuant to Article 209, transfer appropriations from one chapter to another or from one subdivision to another.

Article 205a [1]
The Commission shall submit annually to the Council and to the European Parliament the accounts of the preceding financial year relating to the implementation of the budget. The Commission shall also forward to them a financial statement of the assets and liabilities of the Community.

1 Aa added by the Financial Provisions Treaty, art 14.

Article 206 [1]
1. A Court of Auditors is hereby established.

2. The Court of Auditors shall consist of 12 members.

3. The members of the Court of Auditors shall be chosen from among persons who belong or have belonged in their respective countries to external audit bodies or who are especially qualified for this office. Their independence must be beyond doubt.

4. The members of the Court of Auditors shall be appointed for a term of six years by the Council, acting unanimously after consulting the European Parliament.

However, when the first appointments are made, four members of the Court of Auditors, chosen by lot, shall be appointed for a term of office of four years only.

The members of the Court of Auditors shall be eligible for re-appointment.

They shall elect the President of the Court of Auditors from among their number for a term of three years. The President may be re-elected.

5. The members of the Court of Auditors shall, in the general interest of the Community, be completely independent in the performance of their duties.

In the performance of these duties, they shall neither seek nor take instructions from any government or from any other body. They shall refrain from any action incompatible with their duties.

6. The members of the Court of Auditors may not, during their term of office, engage in any other occupation, whether gainful or not. When entering upon their duties they shall give a solemn undertaking that, both during and after their term of office, they will respect the obligations arising therefrom and in particular their duty to behave with integrity and discretion as regards the acceptance, after they have ceased to hold office, of certain appointments or benefits.

7. Apart from normal replacement, or death, the duties of a member of the Court of Auditors shall end when he resigns, or is compulsorily retired by a ruling of the Court of Justice pursuant to paragraph 8.

The vacancy thus caused shall be filled for the remainder of the member's term of office.

Save in the case of compulsory retirement, members of the Court of Auditors shall remain in office until they have been replaced.

8. A member of the Court of Auditors may be deprived of his office or of his

right to a pension or other benefits in its stead only if the Court of Justice, at the request of the Court of Auditors finds that he no longer fulfils the requisite conditions or meets the obligations arising from his office.

9. The Council, acting by a qualified majority, shall determine the conditions of employment of the President and the members of the Court of Auditors and in particular their salaries, allowances and pensions. It shall also, by the same majority, determine any payment to be made instead of remuneration.

10. The provisions of the Protocol on the Privileges and Immunities of the European Communities applicable to the Judges of the Court of Justice shall also apply to the members of the Court of Auditors.

1 As substituted by the Financial Provisions Treaty, art 15 .

Article 206a [1]
1. The Court of Auditors shall examine the accounts of all revenue and expenditure of the Community. It shall also examine the accounts of all revenue and expenditure of all bodies set up by the Community in so far as the relevant constituent instrument does not preclude such examination.

2. The Court of Auditors shall examine whether all revenue has been received and all expenditure incurred in a lawful and regular manner and whether the financial management has been sound.

The audit of revenue shall be carried out on the basis both of the amounts established as due and the amounts actually paid to the Community.

The audit of expenditure shall be carried out on the basis both of commitments undertaken and payments made.

These audits may be carried out before the closure of accounts for the financial year in question.

3. The audit shall be based on records and, if necessary, performed on the spot in the institutions of the Community and in the Member States. In the Member States the audit shall be carried out in liaison with the national audit bodies or, if these do not have the necessary powers, with the competent national departments. These bodies or departments shall inform the Court of Auditors whether they intend to take part in the audit.

The institutions of the Community and the national audit bodies or, if these do not have the necessary powers, the competent national departments, shall forward to the Court of Auditors, at its request, any document or information necessary to carry out its task.

4. The Court of Auditors shall draw up an annual report after the close of each financial year. It shall be forwarded to the institutions of the Community and shall be published, together with the replies of these institutions to the observations of the Court of Auditors, in the *Official Journal of the European Communities.*

The Court of Auditors may also, at any time, submit observations on specific questions and deliver opinions at the request of one of the institutions of the Community.

It shall adopt its annual reports or opinions by a majority of its members.

It shall assist the European Parliament and the Council in exercising their powers of control over the implementation of the budget.

1 Added by the Financial Provisions Treaty, art 16.

Article 206b [1]

The European Parliament, acting on a recommendation from the Council which shall act by a qualified majority, shall give a discharge to the Commission in respect of the implementation of the budget. To this end, the Council and the European Parliament in turn shall examine the accounts and the financial statement referred to in Article 205a and the annual report by the Court of Auditors together with the replies of the institutions under audit to the observations of the Court of Auditors.

1 Added by the Financial Provisions Treaty, art 17.

Article 207

The budget shall be drawn up in the unit of account determined in accordance with the provisions of the regulations made pursuant to Article 209.

The financial contributions provided for in Article 200 (1) shall be placed at the disposal of the Community by the Member States in their national currencies.

The available balances of these contributions shall be deposited with the Treasuries of Member States or with bodies designated by them. While on deposit, such funds shall retain the value corresponding to the parity, at the date of deposit, in relation to the unit of account referred to in the first paragraph.

The balances may be invested on terms to be agreed between the Commission and the Member State concerned.

The regulations made pursuant to Article 209 shall lay down the technical conditions under which financial operations relating to the European Social Fund shall be carried out.

Article 208

The Commission may, provided it notifies the competent authorities of the Member States concerned, transfer into the currency of one of the Member States its holdings in the currency of another Member State, to the extent necessary to enable them to be used for purposes which come within the scope of this Treaty. The Commission shall as far as possible avoid making such transfers if it possesses cash or liquid assets in the currencies which it needs.

The Commission shall deal with each Member State through the authority designated by the State concerned. In carrying out financial operations the Commission shall employ the services of the bank of issue of the Member State concerned or of any other financial institution approved by that State.

Article 209 [1]

The Council, acting unanimously on a proposal from the Commission and after consulting the European Parliament and obtaining the opinion of the Court of Auditors, shall:

(a) make Financial Regulations specifying in particular the procedure to be adopted for establishing and implementing the budget and for presenting and auditing accounts;

(b) determine the methods and procedure whereby the budget revenue provided under the arrangements relating to the Communities' own resources shall be made available to the Commission, and determine the measures to be applied, if need be, to meet cash requirements;

(c) lay down rules concerning the responsibility of authorising officers and accounting officers and concerning appropriate arrangements for inspection.

1 As substituted by the Financial Provisions Treaty, art 18.

PART SIX

GENERAL AND FINAL PROVISIONS

Article 210
The Community shall have legal personality.

Article 211
In each of the Member States, the Community shall enjoy the most extensive legal capacity accorded to legal persons under their laws; it may, in particular, acquire or dispose of movable and immovable property and may be a party to legal proceedings. To this end, the Community shall be represented by the Commission.

Article 212 ¹

1 Repealed by the Merger Treaty, art 24 (2).

Article 213
The Commission may, within the limits and under the conditions laid down by the Council in accordance with the provisions of this Treaty, collect any information and carry out any checks required for the performance of the tasks entrusted to it.

Article 214
The members of the institutions of the Community, the members of committees, and the officials and other servants of the Community shall be required, even, after their duties have ceased, not to disclose information of the kind covered by the obligation of professional secrecy, in particular information about undertakings, their business relations or their cost components.

Article 215
The contractual liability of the Community shall be governed by the law applicable to the contract in question.

In the case of non-contractual liability, the Community shall, in accordance with the general principles common to the laws of the Member States, make good any damage caused by its institutions or by its servants in the performance of their duties.

The personal liability of its servants towards the Community shall be governed by the provisions laid down in their Staff Regulations or in the Conditions of Employment applicable to them.

Article 216
The seat of the institutions of the Community shall be determined by common accord of the Governments of the Member States.

Article 217
The rules governing the languages of the institutions of the Community shall, without prejudice to the provisions contained in the rules of procedure of the Court of Justice, be determined by the Council, acting unanimously.

Article 218 ¹

1 Repealed by the Merger Treaty, art 28.

Article 219
Member States undertake not to submit a dispute concerning the interpretation or application of this Treaty to any method of settlement other than those provided for therein.

Article 220
Member States shall, so far as is necessary, enter into negotiations with each other with a view to securing for the benefit of their nationals:
- the protection of persons and the enjoyment and protection of rights under the same conditions as those accorded by each State to its own nationals;
- the abolition of double taxation within the Community;
- the mutual recognition of companies or firms within the meaning of the second paragraph of Article 58, the retention of legal personality in the event of transfer of their seat from one country to another, and the possibility of mergers between companies or firms governed by the laws of different countries;
- the simplification of formalities governing the reciprocal recognition and enforcement of judgments of courts or tribunals and of arbitration awards.

Article 221
Within three years of the entry into force of this Treaty, Member States shall accord nationals of the other Member States the same treatment as their own nationals as regards participation in the capital of companies or firms within the meaning of Article 58, without prejudice to the application of the other provisions of this Treaty.

Article 222
This Treaty shall in no way prejudice the rules in Member States governing the system of property ownership.

Article 223
1. The provisions of this Treaty shall not preclude the application of the following rules:
> (a)   No Member State shall be obliged to supply information the disclosure of which it considers contrary to the essential interests of its security;
> (b)   Any Member State may take such measures as it considers necessary for the protection of the essential interests of its security which are connected with the production of or trade in arms, munitions and war material; such measures shall not adversely affect the conditions of competition in the common market regarding products which are not intended for specifically military purposes.

2. During the first year after the entry into force of this Treaty, the Council shall, acting unanimously, draw up a list of products to which the provisions of paragraph 1(b) shall apply.

3. The Council may, acting unanimously on a proposal from the Commission, make changes in this list.

Article 224
Member States shall consult each other with a view to taking together the steps needed to prevent the functioning of the common market being affected by measures which a Member State may be called upon to take in the event

of serious internal disturbances affecting the maintenance of law and order, in the event of war, serious international tension constituting a threat of war, or in order to carry out obligations it has accepted for the purpose of maintaining peace and international security.

Article 225
If measures taken in the circumstances referred to in Articles 223 and 224 have the effect of distorting the conditions of competition in the common market, the Commission shall, together with the State concerned, examine how these measures can be adjusted to the rules laid down in this Treaty.

By way of derogation from the procedure laid down in Articles 169 and 170, the Commission or any Member State may bring the matter directly before the Court of Justice if it considers that another Member State is making improper use of the powers provided for in Articles 223 and 224. The Court of Justice shall give its ruling *in camera*.

Article 226
1. If, during the transitional period, difficulties arise which are serious and liable to persist in any sector of the economy or which could bring about serious deterioration in the economic situation of a given area, a Member State may apply for authorisation to take protective measures in order to rectify the situation and adjust the sector concerned to the economy of the common market.

2. On application by the State concerned, the Commission shall, by emergency procedure, determine without delay the protective measures which it considers necessary, specifying the circumstances and the manner in which they are to be put into effect.

3. The measures authorised under paragraph 2 may involve derogations from the rules of this Treaty, to such an extent and for such periods as are strictly necessary in order to attain the objectives referred to in paragraph 1. Priority shall be given to such measures as will least disturb the functioning of the common market.

Article 227
1. This Treaty shall apply to the Kingdom of Belgium, the Kingdom of Denmark, the Federal Republic of Germany, the Hellenic Republic, the Kingdom of Spain, the French Republic, Ireland, the Italian Republic, the Grand Duchy of Luxembourg, the Kingdom of the Netherlands, the Portuguese Republic and the United Kingdom of Great Britain and Northern Ireland.[1]

2. With regard to Algeria and the French overseas departments, the general and particular provisions of this Treaty relating to:
- the free movement of goods;
- agriculture, save for Article 40(4);
- the liberalisation of services;
- the rules on competition;
- the protective measures provided for in Articles 108, 109 and 226;
- the institutions;
shall apply as soon as this Treaty enters into force.

The conditions under which the other provisions of this Treaty are to apply shall be determined, within two years of the entry into force of this Treaty, by decisions of the Council, acting unanimously on a proposal from the Commission.

The institutions of the Community will, within the framework of the procedures provided for in this Treaty, in particular Article 226, take care that the economic and social development of these areas is made possible.

3. The special arrangements for association set out in Part Four of this Treaty shall apply to the overseas countries and territories listed in Annex, IV to this Treaty.

This Treaty shall not apply to those overseas countries and territories having special relations with the United Kingdom of Great Britain and Northern Ireland which are not included in the aforementioned list.

4. The provisions of this Treaty shall apply to the European territories for whose external relations a Member State is responsible.

5. Notwithstanding the preceding paragraphs:
   (a)   This Treaty shall not apply to the Faroe Islands. The Government of the Kingdom of Denmark may, however, give notice, by a declaration deposited by 31 December 1975 at the latest with the Government of the Italian Republic, which shall transmit a certified copy thereof to each of the Governments of the other Member States, that this Treaty shall apply to those Islands. In that event, this Treaty shall apply to those Islands from the first day of the second month following the deposit of the declaration.
   (b)   This Treaty shall not apply to the Sovereign Base Areas of the United Kingdom of Great Britain and Northern Ireland in Cyprus.
   (c)   This Treaty shall apply to the Channel Islands and the Isle of Man only to the extent necessary to ensure the implementation of the arrangements for those islands set out in the Treaty concerning the accession of new Member States to the European Economic Community and to the European Atomic Energy Community signed on 22 January 1972.[1]

1 As amended by the First and Third Acts of Accession.

Article 228
1. Where this Treaty provides for the conclusion of agreements between the Community and one or more States or an international organisation, such agreements shall be negotiated by the Commission. Subject to the powers vested in the Commission in this field, such agreements shall be concluded by the Council, after consulting the European Parliament where required by this Treaty.

The Council, the Commission or a Member State may obtain beforehand the opinion of the Court of Justice as to whether an agreement envisaged is compatible with the provisions of this Treaty. Where the opinion of the Court of Justice is adverse, the agreement may enter into force only in accordance with Article 236.

2. Agreements concluded under these conditions shall be binding on the institutions of the Community and on Member States.

Article 229
It shall be for the Commission to ensure the maintenance of all appropriate relations with the organs of the United Nations, of its specialised agencies and of the General Agreement on Tariffs and Trade.

The Commission shall also maintain such relations as are appropriate with all international organisations.

Article 230
The Community shall establish all appropriate forms of co-operation with the Council of Europe.

Article 231

The Community shall establish close co-operation with the Organisation for European Economic Co-operation, the details to be determined by common accord.

Article 232

1. The provisions of this Treaty shall not affect the provisions of the Treaty establishing the European Coal and Steel Community, in particular as regards the rights and obligations of Member States, the powers of the institutions of that Community and the rules laid down by that Treaty for the functioning of the common market in coal and steel.

2. The provisions of this Treaty shall not derogate from those of the Treaty establishing the European Atomic Energy Community.

Article 233

The provisions of this Treaty shall not preclude the existence or completion of regional unions between Belgium and Luxembourg, or between Belgium, Luxembourg and the Netherlands, to the extent that the objectives of these regional unions are not attained by application of this Treaty.

Article 234

The rights and obligations arising from agreements concluded before the entry into force of this Treaty between one or more Member States on the one hand, and one or more third countries on the other, shall not be affected by the provisions of this Treaty.

To the extent that such agreements are not compatible with this Treaty, the Member State or States concerned shall take all appropriate steps to eliminate the incompatibilities established. Member States shall, where necessary, assist each other to this end and shall, where appropriate, adopt a common attitude.

In applying the agreements referred to in the first paragraph, Member States shall take into account the fact that the advantages accorded under this Treaty by each Member State form an integral part of the establishment of the Community and are thereby inseparably linked with the creation of common institutions, the conferring of powers upon them and the granting of the same advantages by all the other Member States.

Article 235

If action by the Community should prove necessary to attain, in the course of the operation of the common market, one of the objectives of the Community and this Treaty has not provided the necessary powers, the Council shall, acting unanimously on a proposal from the Commission and after consulting the European Parliament, take the appropriate measures.

Article 236

The Government of any Member State or the Commission may submit to the Council proposals for the amendment of this Treaty.

If the Council, after consulting the European Parliament and, where appropriate, the Commission, delivers an opinion in favour of calling a conference of representatives of the Governments of the Member States, the conference shall be convened by the President of the Council for the purpose of determining by common accord the amendments to be made to this Treaty.

The amendments shall enter into force after being ratified by all the Member States in accordance with their respective constitutional requirements.

Article 237

Any European State may apply to become a member of the Community. It shall address its application to the Council, which shall act unanimously after consulting the Commission and after receiving the assent of the European Parliament which shall act by an absolute majority of its component members.[1]

The conditions of admission and the adjustments to this Treaty necessitated thereby shall be the subject of an agreement between the Member States and the applicant State. This agreement shall be submitted for ratification by all the Contracting States in accordance with their respective constitutional requirements.

1 As amended by the Single European Act, art 8.

Article 238

The Community may conclude with a third State, a union of States or an international organisation agreements establishing an association involving reciprocal rights and obligations, common action and special procedures.

These agreements shall be concluded by the Council, acting unanimously and after receiving the assent of the European Parliament which shall act by an absolute majority of its component members.[1]

Where such agreements call for amendments to this Treaty, these amendments shall first be adopted in accordance with the procedure laid down in Article 236.

1 As amended by the Single Eurpoean Act, art 9.

Article 239

The Protocols annexed to this Treaty by common accord of the Member States shall form an integral part thereof.

Article 240

This Treaty is concluded for an unlimited period.

SETTING UP OF THE INSTITUTIONS

Article 241

The Council shall meet within one month of the entry into force of this Treaty.

Article 242

The Council shall, within three months of its first meeting. take all appropriate measures to constitute the Economic and Social Committee.

Article 243

The Assembly shall meet within two months of the first meeting of the Council, having been convened by the President of the Council, in order to elect its officers and draw up its rules of procedure. Pending the election of its officers, the oldest member shall take the chair.

Article 244

The Court of Justice shall take up its duties as soon as its members have been appointed. Its first President shall be appointed for three years in the same manner as its members.

The Court of Justice shall adopt its rules of procedure within three months of taking up its duties.

No matter may be brought before the Court of Justice until its rules of procedure have been published. The time within which an action must be brought shall run only from the date of this publication.

Upon his appointment, the President of the Court of Justice shall exercise the powers conferred upon him by this Treaty.

Article 245
The Commission shall take up its duties and assume the responsibilities conferred upon it by this Treaty as soon as its members have been appointed.

Upon taking up its duties, the Commission shall undertake the studies and arrange the contacts needed for making an overall survey of the economic situation of the Community.

Article 246
1. The first financial year shall run from the date on which this Treaty enters into force until 31 December following. Should this Treaty, however, enter into force during the second half of the year, the first financial year shall run until 31 December of the following year.

2. Until the budget for the first financial year has been established, Member States shall make the Community interest-free advances which shall be deducted from their financial contributions to the implementation of the budget.

3. Until the Staff Regulations of officials and the Conditions of Employment of other servants of the Community provided for in Article 212 have been laid down, each institution shall recruit the staff it needs and to this end conclude contracts of limited duration.

Each institution shall examine together with the Council any question concerning the number, remuneration and distribution of posts.

FINAL PROVISIONS

Article 247
This Treaty shall be ratified by the High Contracting Parties in accordance with their respective constitutional requirements. The instruments of ratification shall be deposited with the Government of the Italian Republic.

This Treaty shall enter into force on the first day of the month following the deposit of the instrument of ratification by the last signatory State to take this step. If, however, such deposit is made less than fifteen days before the beginning of the following month, this Treaty shall not enter into force until the first day of the second month after the date of such deposit.

Article 248
This Treaty, drawn up in a single original in the Dutch, French, German and Italian languages, all four texts being equally authentic, shall be deposited in the archives of the Government of the Italian Republic, which shall transmit a certified copy to each of the Governments of the other signatory States.

Rome,
25 March 1957.

INDEX

Index